Healthy Heart
COOKBOOK

KEEPING YOUR HEART HEALTHY

FOOD PLAYS A CRITICAL ROLE IN PREVENTING AND MANAGING HEART DISEASE. IN FACT, EATING A DIET THAT IS LOW IN UNHEALTHY FATS; IS RICH IN WHOLE GRAINS, FRUITS, VEGETABLES, AND FIBER; AND INCLUDES HEART-PROTECTING omega-3 fatty acids can actually lower your risk of heart disease. Knowing that what you eat can influence your chances of developing heart disease is important because it means you may actually be able to control your risk.

Consuming too many saturated fats, for example, raises blood cholesterol levels. In some people, a high sodium intake can elevate blood pressure. Eating more calories than your body burns causes weight gain, which sets the stage for diabetes and high blood pressure. All of these—high cholesterol, high blood pressure, being overweight, and having diabetes— are important risk factors for heart disease.

The American Medical Association Healthy Heart Cookbook is an indispensable source for people with heart disease and those at risk of developing it—and for anyone who wants to eat healthy dishes that taste good. The book makes it easy to choose nutritious foods for yourself and your family every day by offering delicious dishes that are easy to prepare.

UNDERSTANDING HEART DISEASE

Heart disease is the number one killer of both men and women in the United States. Some people are more likely than others to develop heart disease. Several risk factors—such as age, family history, and ethnic background—cannot be changed, but others, especially lifestyle choices such as smoking, diet, and activity level, are under your control.

Disease-fighting foods (facing page, clockwise from top left): onions, high in compounds that lower cholesterol; fresh salad greens, rich in vitamins; salmon, a source of heart-healthy omega-3 fatty acids; and corn on the cob, a healthful vegetable.

How heart disease starts

Heart disease—also known as coronary artery disease—begins when a fatty substance called plaque builds up in the walls of the blood vessels that supply blood to the heart. This condition, called atherosclerosis, or hardening of the arteries, develops gradually over many years and can even start during childhood.

Eventually, the arteries can narrow and reduce the amount of blood and oxygen that reach the heart, causing chest pain called angina. Pieces of plaque can break away from the artery wall and form a clot that reduces blood flow to the heart even more.

If a clot suddenly blocks an artery that supplies blood to an area of the heart, you experience what's called a heart attack. During a heart attack, cells in the heart muscle that fail to get enough oxygen-rich blood begin to die. The more time that passes before medical treatment to restore adequate blood flow, the greater the damage to the heart.

Diet and heart disease

Your diet is one of the most powerful influences on your risk of heart disease. Simply reducing your consumption of fatty foods and eating more high-fiber vegetables, fruits, whole grains, and legumes can significantly improve the health of your blood vessels and heart.

Warning signs of a heart attack

The classic symptom of a heart attack is crushing or squeezing pain in the center of the chest, but pain can also occur in the left arm, jaw, neck, or back. The symptoms can be hard to identify because a heart attack can feel different to different people. Women, especially, can experience other symptoms with or without chest pain. For example, women are more likely than men to experience dizziness, nausea, weakness, sweating, and fainting during a heart attack. If you think you or someone else may be having a heart attack, call 911 or your local emergency number for help immediately.

FIGHTING HEART DISEASE

You may have bought this book because you have heart disease or because you want to avoid it. No matter what the state of your health, your chances of having a heart attack can be influenced by several things you control—your diet, how much you exercise, whether you smoke, your weight, and your ability to deal with stress.

All-in-one dishes such as Szechuan Noodles with Shredded Beef (page 84) make excellent heart-healthy fare, combining whole grains and fresh vegetables with lean meat.

Biking and walking (facing page) are simple activities that can help people lower their blood pressure and cholesterol levels.

Eat a heart-healthy diet

To keep your heart healthy, eat a diet abundant in fruits, vegetables, whole grains, and legumes—foods in the recipes in this book. Fruits and vegetables contain lots of vitamins and minerals, including antioxidants (see "A Dose of Protection," page 13).

Fruits and vegetables, along with legumes and whole-grain breads and breakfast cereals, are also rich in fiber, especially soluble fiber, which protects your heart by lowering your blood cholesterol and glucose levels. In smaller amounts, unsaturated fats (such as those found in olive oil, canola oil, avocados, and nuts), lean meat and poultry, fish, and fat-free dairy products are also heart-healthy.

Foods that can harm your heart—and should thus be limited or avoided—include those made with refined flours and sugar, fried foods, salty foods, and foods that contain saturated and trans fats (such as pastries, salty snacks, fatty meats, poultry skin, and french fries).

Get plenty of exercise

Scientific evidence points to the many benefits of regular physical activity. Frequent exercise can cut your risk of heart disease by a third—by lowering your blood pressure, improving your cholesterol profile (by reducing total cholesterol and raising beneficial HDL cholesterol), helping to keep your weight down, and relieving stress.

Try to exercise for at least 30 to 60 minutes every day. The time you devote to exercise doesn't have to be continuous. You can break up your activity into two 15-minute and three 10-minute sessions, for example, and get the same benefits you would from one long exercise session.

Walking is excellent exercise, especially if you have been inactive, but the more vigorous the activity, the more your heart will benefit. Fit more exercise into your daily routine by, for example, taking the stairs instead of the elevator and parking farther from the store or office.

CONTENTS

American Medical Association

Healthy Heart
COOKBOOK

RECIPES
Cheryl Forberg, R.D.

PHOTOGRAPHS
Jim Franco
Sheri Giblin

MEREDITH® BOOKS
Des Moines, Iowa

Don't smoke

Not only does cigarette smoking increase your risk of lung cancer and emphysema, it is also a major contributor to heart disease. Nicotine triggers the release of the stress hormone adrenaline, causing your blood vessels to narrow, your heart to beat faster, and your blood pressure to rise.

Carbon monoxide in cigarette smoke competes with oxygen for space in red blood cells, reducing the heart's supply of oxygen. It also promotes blood clots and plaque in the arteries. Secondhand smoke can harm nonsmokers, especially children.

The good news is that your risk of heart disease is cut in half one year after quitting. In 5 to 15 years, your risk equals that of a nonsmoker.

Maintain a healthy weight

Carrying too much weight elevates your blood pressure and can lead to type 2 diabetes, a major risk factor for heart disease. Losing as few as 10 pounds can help reduce this risk.

Avoid fad diets and programs that eliminate whole food groups such as carbohydrates; they can harm your health. The real key is simply to burn more calories than you consume.

Reduce stress

Stress makes your heart beat faster, increases the amount of harmful LDL cholesterol in your bloodstream, raises your blood sugar level, and increases the blood's tendency to clot. If you feel overstressed, talk to your doctor about steps you can take.

SHOULD YOU TAKE HEART MEDICATION?

Based on a person's risk factors and health profile, doctors may prescribe drugs to prevent or treat heart disease.

• Chest pain (angina) can be treated with beta blockers (to ease the heart's workload), nitroglycerin (to widen blood vessels), and calcium channel blockers (to relax arteries). Beta blockers may be prescribed for people who have had a heart attack.

• Blood clotting can be inhibited with aspirin, anticoagulants, and platelet inhibitors.

• Blood cholesterol levels that don't improve with diet changes, exercise, and weight loss are usually treated with statins. Statins lower LDL (bad) cholesterol and total cholesterol.

SETTING NUTRITION GOALS

Although recommendations for heart-healthy eating vary widely—some advocate traditional Mediterranean or Asian diets, for instance—there are a number of simple, research-based guidelines that apply to everyone hoping to avoid a heart attack or stroke.

To lower your risk, consume a balanced diet that is low in calories, saturated and trans fats, salt, sugar, and alcohol. Choose whole grains over refined ones and add high-fiber vegetables, fruits, and legumes. The recipes in this book can help you follow these guidelines.

The food you eat is composed of carbohydrates, fats, and protein. Carbohydrates and fats are your body's main sources of fuel. Carbs should make up 45 to 65 percent of your daily calories, fats (primarily from vegetable fats) about 20 to 35 percent, and protein about 12 to 20 percent.

HOW TO DISTRIBUTE YOUR DAILY CALORIES

45–65%
Carbohydrates

20–35%
Fats

12–20%
Protein

CARBOHYDRATES

Carbohydrates are the many kinds of sugars, starches, and fibers that make up plant foods such as fruits, vegetables, and whole grains (the seeds of grasses). Overall, these carbohydrates are some of the healthiest foods you can eat. When it comes to fighting heart disease, however, whole grains and fiber are especially beneficial.

Whole grains

The world's great cuisines are built on grains—wheat, oats, rice, corn, rye, barley, buckwheat, millet, kasha, and quinoa. Whole grains are rich in B vitamins, notably folic acid, which may lower heart disease risk. They also supply minerals such as calcium, magnesium, and phosphorus.

Refined carbohydrates

Grains stripped of their brown outer husk lose most of their nutrients and fiber. For this reason, multigrain breads, whole-wheat pastas, brown rice, and oat and bran cereals are superior to white bread and other products made from refined grains.

Two fibers, two benefits

Soluble fiber helps lower heart disease risk by reducing cholesterol and blood sugar levels. It is plentiful in legumes, oats, barley, and some vegetables and fruits. Insoluble fiber makes you feel full and helps protect against digestive problems.

A DOSE OF PROTECTION

Fruits and vegetables are excellent sources of antioxidant vitamins that fight free-radical damage to the lining of arteries and are linked to a reduced risk of heart disease, high blood pressure, and stroke.

Fruits and vegetables also contain many other disease-fighting compounds called phytochemicals, more and more of which are being discovered every day.

Because phytochemicals and antioxidants boost each other's effectiveness in fighting disease, try to eat foods containing a variety of them every day. Aim for a minimum of five servings of vegetables and fruits a day—ten is even better.

HEALTHY FATS

Fats in food transport some vitamins through the bloodstream and help your body store energy. They make food taste smooth and creamy and help make you feel full. Oils from nuts, seeds, and vegetables as well as fats from seafoods provide health benefits and can reduce your risk of heart disease. These fats, known as unsaturated fats, are usually liquid.

Heart-healthy monounsaturated fats add satisfying richness to the salad Grapefruit & Avocado with Cilantro Cream (page 53).

Monounsaturated fats

Olive, canola, and peanut oils are the main sources of monounsaturated fats, the healthiest fats you can eat. They lower LDL (the so-called bad cholesterol) and raise HDL (good cholesterol) in the blood, helping lower heart disease risk.

Polyunsaturated fats

These fats, which are essential for good health, include corn, sunflower, safflower, flaxseed, and soybeans oils, as well as the oils in fatty fish such as salmon. Rich in omega-3 and omega-6 fatty acids, they lower total cholesterol (but also cut HDL cholesterol).

Plant sterols

Nuts, seeds, and many other plant foods contain substances called plant sterols that slow the absorption of dietary cholesterol and can lower LDL and total cholesterol levels in the blood. Soft margarines and salad dressings with added plant sterols are available in most stores.

HARMFUL FATS

Foods high in saturated and trans fats can increase your risk for heart disease and some forms of cancer. These kinds of fats are usually solid or semisolid at room temperature, although they may turn liquid when heated. It's not possible to avoid all harmful fats because they occur in many foods, but it's best to cut back wherever you can.

Saturated fats

Plentiful in meat, dark-meat poultry and poultry skin, butter, full-fat dairy products, coconut oil, and palm oil, saturated fats increase total blood cholesterol and LDL (bad) cholesterol. Limit these fats, along with trans fats, to no more than 8 to 10 percent of your total daily calories.

Trans fats

Stick margarine and shortening contain hydrogenated oils that raise total blood cholesterol and LDL cholesterol levels. Called trans fats, they are also common in packaged and processed foods, baked goods, and fried foods such as french fries.

Cholesterol

Egg yolks, liver, shellfish, and full-fat dairy products are rich in cholesterol, which can raise blood cholesterol, although it does not do so in all people. Saturated and trans fats have a greater impact on blood cholesterol than does dietary cholesterol.

PROTEIN

Protein, an essential nutrient found in both plant and animal foods, repairs tissues, builds muscle, and carries hormones and vitamins throughout the body via the bloodstream. Infants and growing children have the highest daily protein requirements, but most Americans consume far more protein than they actually need.

HOW MUCH PROTEIN IS ENOUGH?

Adults need a surprisingly small quantity of protein every day—only 0.8 grams of protein per kilogram (2.2 pounds) of body weight.

There are almost 30 grams of protein in a 3-ounce chicken breast and in a 2-cup bowl of black bean soup. Use your weight to determine how much protein you may need in a day, following the chart below.

140 pounds	—	51 grams
150 pounds	—	55 grams
160 pounds	—	59 grams
170 pounds	—	62 grams
180 pounds	—	65 grams

People whose meals are low in fat and protein and rich in plant foods, as in many developing countries, have a significantly lower incidence of heart disease than do Americans, who typically consume more foods high in protein, fat, and calories.

Red meats and poultry

Beef, pork, lamb, chicken, and turkey are protein-rich foods that often contain large amounts of harmful saturated fats (page 15), although lean cuts are available. The portions of foods such as beef and chicken in this cookbook are relatively small.

Legumes and fish

Plant proteins such as beans, lentils, peas, and nuts contain healthier fats than do animal proteins, have no cholesterol, and provide healthful fiber. Fish, also a fine protein source, has about as much protein as lean beef, ounce for ounce, but also supplies heart-healthy omega-3 fatty acids.

High-protein diets

Low-carbohydrate, high-protein, high-fat diets can result in rapid weight loss but may increase the risk of kidney damage and brittle bones, or osteoporosis. Talk to your doctor or a dietitian if you are thinking about trying a high-protein diet.

SALT

High blood pressure is a major risk factor for heart disease. In many people, blood pressure rises dangerously when they consume too much of the mineral sodium, principally from the salt added to foods.

Going low sodium

If you have high blood pressure, your doctor may have asked you to lower your intake of sodium. But limiting sodium means more than just putting away the salt shaker. It also means staying away from most fast foods and highly salted packaged and canned foods, such as canned soups and the flavor packets that come with packaged rice dishes.

FLAVOR ENHANCERS

Experiment with herbs and spices, lemon and lime juices, garlic and onion powders, and other sodium-free seasonings. Read food labels carefully to find out exactly how much salt a serving of packaged food provides. Buy reduced-sodium or salt-free canned vegetables and snack foods such as pretzels.

ALCOHOL

Although a link has been found between moderate drinking and a reduced risk of heart attack, doctors are not recommending that people start drinking wine or other alcoholic beverages for their health.

Alcohol's effect on the heart

Although alcohol's protective effect is not fully understood, doctors do know that in moderate amounts alcohol raises the blood level of HDL cholesterol (which cleanses the arteries of harmful LDL cholesterol) and reduces the formation of blood clots (which can block arteries and trigger heart attacks and strokes).

WHAT'S MODERATE?

Moderate drinking is one drink a day for women and two a day for men. A drink is the equivalent of one 5-ounce glass of wine, a 12-ounce beer, or 1½ ounces of liquor. Heavy drinking can damage the blood vessels and the heart and can increase the risk of high blood pressure, heart attack, and stroke.

KEEPING FAT UNDER CONTROL

Because saturated and trans fats have the more harmful influences on your blood cholesterol, your doctor may suggest cutting back on the amount of these fats you eat each day. Although some fats are beneficial, the easiest way to cut back on the two harmful fats is to reduce your intake of all fats. Follow the three easy steps in the next few pages to estimate your needs.

HOW TO FIND THE NUTRIENT VALUES IN EACH RECIPE

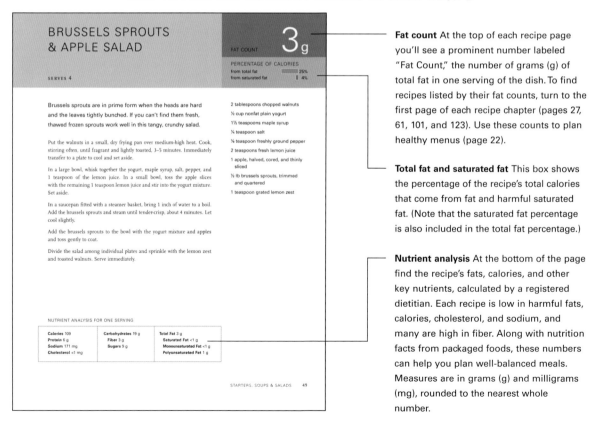

Fat count At the top of each recipe page you'll see a prominent number labeled "Fat Count," the number of grams (g) of total fat in one serving of the dish. To find recipes listed by their fat counts, turn to the first page of each recipe chapter (pages 27, 61, 101, and 123). Use these counts to plan healthy menus (page 22).

Total fat and saturated fat This box shows the percentage of the recipe's total calories that come from fat and harmful saturated fat. (Note that the saturated fat percentage is also included in the total fat percentage.)

Nutrient analysis At the bottom of the page find the recipe's fats, calories, and other key nutrients, calculated by a registered dietitian. Each recipe is low in harmful fats, calories, cholesterol, and sodium, and many are high in fiber. Along with nutrition facts from packaged foods, these numbers can help you plan well-balanced meals. Measures are in grams (g) and milligrams (mg), rounded to the nearest whole number.

1 NOTE YOUR ACTIVITY LEVEL

Your activity level and weight together determine the amount of food you should eat. The more frequent and intense your activities, the more food energy—calories—you burn. Of course, everyday activities such as shopping take less energy than exercise such as jogging. Read the descriptions below to find the one that best describes your activity level.

Take your activity level and go to step 2 →

INACTIVE
Mainly sedentary most days of the week. Daily activities limited to driving, reading, watching television, and cooking, with only rare, light exertion such as shopping.

SOMEWHAT ACTIVE
Low-intensity activity throughout the week. Activities include light housework, leisurely walks, playing with children, climbing stairs at home, low-intensity sports such as golf or bowling.

ACTIVE
Vigorous exercise several days a week. Activities include long brisk walks or bike rides, gardening, mid-intensity sports such as tennis, skiing, softball, swimming, dancing, or yoga.

CAN IRON CONTRIBUTE TO HEART DISEASE?

A high level of iron in the blood is a newly recognized risk factor for heart disease. Excess iron may damage the arteries that supply blood to the heart, promoting the buildup of artery-clogging plaque.

Doctors believe this explains why men who donate blood regularly and women who menstruate are less likely than other people to develop heart disease.

Although iron is an essential mineral, you don't need very much. Red meats as well as iron-fortified breakfast cereals and breads usually supply sufficient amounts.

If you're either a male or a non-menstruating female, you should avoid taking supplements with iron unless your doctor suggests them.

Activity's benefits

Regular exercise can help you lower your heart attack risk. Inactive and somewhat active people who increase their weekly activity even a little reap many health benefits, including improved blood cholesterol levels, lower blood pressure, sounder sleep, more upbeat mood, increased alertness, and improved memory—and they tend to lose weight. Talk to your doctor about the right type and amount of activity for you.

2 FIND YOUR CALORIE NEEDS

The more you weigh, the more calories you need to consume every day. To determine how many calories you can eat each day without gaining or losing pounds, find your weight on the far left side of the chart below; then locate your daily calorie allowance to the right in the column that corresponds to your activity level.

Take your calorie needs and go to step 3 →

LOSE WEIGHT SAFELY

People at risk of heart disease who lose excess weight can lower their cholesterol levels and reduce their heart attack risk. To lose a pound a week—a safe goal—it's necessary to cut about 500 calories a day.

A good approach is to cut back on high-fat, high-sodium, and low-fiber foods and to plan more meals and snacks around whole grains, vegetables, and fruits.

An apple and a chocolate bar can both be satisfying snacks, but the apple is nearly fat-free while the chocolate bar has 15 grams of fat and 150 more calories.

WEIGHT (in pounds)	INACTIVE	SOMEWHAT ACTIVE	ACTIVE
120	1500	1700	1800
130	1600	1800	1900
140	1700	1900	2100
150	1800	2000	2200
160	2000	2100	2400
170	2100	2300	2500
180	2200	2400	2700
190	2300	2500	2800
200	2500	2700	3000
210	2600	2800	3100
220	2700	3000	3300
230	2800	3100	3400
240	2900	3200	3600
250	3100	3300	3700
260	3200	3500	3900
270	3300	3600	4000
280	3400	3700	4100

CALORIES

3 LOCATE YOUR FAT COUNT

For most people, fats should make up about 30 percent of their total daily calories, a level that's actually quite easy to reach. However, your doctor may suggest a lower amount (see "What's Your Fat Percentage?" below right). In the chart below, locate the box with your daily calorie allowance to find the number of grams (g) of fat you can eat in a day.

To use your fat count turn the page →

CALORIES	FAT	CALORIES	FAT	CALORIES	FAT
1500	50g	2400	80g	3300	110g
1600	53g	2500	83g	3400	113g
1700	57g	2600	87g	3500	117g
1800	60g	2700	90g	3600	120g
1900	63g	2800	93g	3700	123g
2000	67g	2900	97g	3800	127g
2100	70g	3000	100g	3900	130g
2200	73g	3100	103g	4000	133g
2300	77g	3200	107g	4100	137g

WHAT'S YOUR FAT PERCENTAGE?

Because you may have special health needs related to fat and cholesterol, your doctor may ask you to adjust the percentage of calories from fat in your diet.

The chart at left shows the number of fat grams that equal 30 percent of total daily calories. If your doctor has suggested eating less, use the following easy formula. Say your daily calorie need is 1800 and your recommended fat percent is 25.

1 Multiply 1800 by 0.25. That equals 450 fat calories per day.

2 Divide your daily fat calories by 9 (the calories in 1 gram of fat). Your daily fat count is 50 grams.

PLANNING HEALTHY MENUS

Your daily fat count may seem like a fairly large number of grams, but remember that a gram is a tiny quantity. There are 14 grams of pure fat in a single tablespoon of olive or canola oil. When you count the fat in salad dressings, cheese, peanut butter, snacks, seafoods, and meats, you'll be surprised how quickly the grams add up.

A sample day's menu

Your fat count is 54 grams and you've decided to spread them between three meals and a snack— roughly 30 percent for each meal and 10 percent for the snack.

Breakfast (per serving)	11 g
2 Banana Bran Muffins (page 125)	8 g
1 cup 1-percent milk	3 g

Lunch (per serving)	15 g
Marinated Corn Salad (page 56)	1 g
Black Bean Quesadillas (page 87)	9 g
Blueberry Gingerbread (page 126)	5 g

Snack (per serving)	8 g
2 PBJ Cookies (page 130)	8 g

Dinner (per serving)	20 g
Chicken with Rosemary & Pearl Onions (page 77)	8 g
Barley Risotto (page 105)	3 g
Spicy Greens with Sun-Dried Tomatoes (page 118)	4 g
Chocolate Hazelnut Biscotti (page 129)	5 g

Day's total	54 g

COOKING FOR GOOD HEALTH

Having healthy ingredients on hand—like low-sodium canned broths and tomatoes in the cupboard, and lean meats and whole-grain bread in the freezer—allows you to put together nutritious meals quickly and easily.

Variety is key

Keep your meals simple but vary your diet by trying new grains, fruits, and vegetables. Experiment with vegetarian dishes. Vegetarians are less likely than meat eaters to develop heart disease, high blood pressure, and obesity, making a meatless diet especially appropriate for people at risk of a heart attack. But you need to plan vegetarian meals carefully to ensure that you get sufficient protein and other essential nutrients.

Smart shopping

Take advantage of the many reduced-fat, fat-free, low-sodium, and sugar-free products now in markets. Stock plenty of fresh, frozen, and canned vegetables and fruits (without added sugar). Seek out unsweetened high-fiber cereals and low-fat cheeses. Shop for salt-free "natural" peanut butter and bypass fatty and salty convenience foods. Check labels to find low-fat foods containing 3 grams of fat or fewer for every 100 calories.

Healthier choices in the kitchen

You know it's wise to choose low-fat dairy products over full-fat ones and whole grains over refined ones. Try these other healthy options.

Replace ground meat with beans or soy protein.

Substitute 2 egg whites for each whole egg.

Use soy milk, rice milk, or nut milk instead of cow's milk.

Replace butter, bacon fat, and lard with canola, olive, or peanut oil.

Use lemon juice or vinegar and herbs and spices in place of salt.

Whip evaporated skim milk instead of heavy cream.

Substitute soft tofu for ricotta cheese.

Marinate poultry and meat in nonfat yogurt instead of oil.

SERVING SIZES

Packaged foods can be confusing. For example, a juice carton may say a serving is 8 ounces, while your recommended serving size is ½ cup, or 4 ounces. Here are some tips for watching how much you eat.

• Use measuring cups and spoons to measure portions, or weigh foods on a kitchen scale.

• Weigh bread slices and bagel halves to make sure they fit into your calorie limit. If they're too large, cut them into smaller pieces.

• Divide and weigh meat and poultry portions before cooking. A 3-ounce piece is the size of a deck of cards.

FOODS THAT FIGHT HEART DISEASE

INGREDIENT	CONTAINS	HEALTH BENEFIT
Oats • legumes • vegetables • dried fruit • whole grains • berries and other fresh fruit	**Fiber**	Helps control weight; promotes healthy digestion; soluble fiber improves cholesterol and lowers blood sugar.
Fruits and vegetables • nuts • vegetable oils • wheat germ • fish and seafood	**Antioxidants**	Fight cell-damaging free radicals, which are produced when blood sugar is high and may contribute to complications of diabetes.
Nuts and seeds • corn and soybean oils • tub margarines with added sterols	**Plant sterols**	Lower cholesterol levels.
Legumes • fish • poultry • lean meats • low-fat dairy products • low-fat tofu	**Low-fat protein**	Builds, maintains, and repairs body tissues.
Salmon • sardines • mackerel • herring • flaxseed and flaxseed oil	**Omega-3 fatty acids**	Reduce heart disease risk by improving cholesterol and preventing blood clots; reduce joint pain and inflammation.
Dark green leafy vegetables • fruits • legumes • wheat germ • whole grains	**Folic acid**	Reduces heart risk by reducing homocysteine in the blood; helps form blood cells; essential in pregnancy for preventing birth defects.

INGREDIENT	CONTAINS	HEALTH BENEFIT
Onions and garlic • chives • shallots • leeks	**Allicin**	A sulfur-containing substance that may lower cholesterol, reduce blood-clotting, and control blood pressure.
Dairy products • fortified juices • fortified breakfast cereals • legumes • canned fish (with bones)	**Calcium**	Essential for transmitting nerve impulses, regulating heart rhythm, and enhancing muscle function; maintains bone strength.
Bran cereals • whole grains • green beans • broccoli • spices • processed meats	**Chromium**	Enhances insulin's effects in converting sugar, protein, and fat into energy; works with insulin to transport sugar from the blood into cells.
Spinach and beet greens • nuts • whole grains • legumes • dairy products • fish • meat • poultry	**Magnesium**	Helps lower blood pressure; helps prevent irregular heartbeat; more is needed when blood sugar is high and when taking diuretics.
Whole grains • sunflower seeds • oysters • gelatin • vegetable oil • corn • parsley • green beans • soy	**Vanadium**	A trace mineral that promotes insulin production and increases the body's sensitivity to insulin.
Shellfish • red meat • legumes • nuts • eggs • tofu and other soy foods • wheat germ	**Zinc**	Needed for the breakdown of protein, fat, and carbohydrates; helps make protein and insulin; essential for growth and development.

STARTERS, SOUPS & SALADS

Tomato & Spinach Soup, 46

FAT COUNT

5g

PERCENTAGE OF CALORIES
from total fat 27%
from saturated fat 3%

WHITE BEAN DIP WITH TORTILLA CHIPS

SERVES 8

1½ cups canned white beans (about one 15-oz can), rinsed and drained

3 cloves garlic, chopped

2 tablespoons olive oil

1 tablespoon fresh lime juice

1 teaspoon chopped jalapeño or chipotle chile (optional)

½ teaspoon ground cumin

½ teaspoon salt

2 tablespoons chopped fresh cilantro

12 stone-ground corn tortillas

Olive oil cooking spray

This creamy high-fiber dip with homemade tortilla chips is a great choice when you need a tasty snack. It takes just minutes to prepare. You can substitute ½ cup dried white beans for the canned beans. (For tips on cooking dried beans, see page 135.)

Place the white beans in a food processor. Add the garlic, olive oil, lime juice, jalapeño (if using), cumin, and ¼ teaspoon of the salt. Process until smooth. Transfer to a bowl and stir in the cilantro. Set aside.

Preheat the oven to 400°F.

Stack the tortillas and cut the stack into 8 wedges to make chips. Spread the tortilla chips in a single layer on a baking sheet, spray lightly with olive oil cooking spray, and sprinkle with the remaining ¼ teaspoon salt. Bake until the chips are crisp and slightly golden, about 10 minutes. Serve with the white bean dip.

NUTRIENT ANALYSIS FOR ONE SERVING

Calories 166	**Carbohydrates** 27 g	**Total Fat** 5 g
Protein 6 g	**Fiber** 4 g	**Saturated Fat** <1 g
Sodium 192 mg	**Sugars** 2 g	**Monounsaturated Fat** 3 g
Cholesterol 0 mg		**Polyunsaturated Fat** <1 g

GRILLED PORK SATAYS WITH PEANUT GLAZE

SERVES 6

Satay is the Asian form of the Mediterranean kabob. For a tasty alternative, try bite-sized pieces of chicken or lean beef instead of pork. If using wooden skewers, soak them in water for about 30 minutes before grilling or broiling to prevent burning.

In a blender or food processor, combine the soy sauce, lime juice, onion, peanut butter, honey, garlic, ginger, cumin, and 1 tablespoon water. Process until smooth. Pour the marinade into a large lock-top plastic bag. Add the pork and refrigerate for 1–2 hours, turning the bag occasionally.

Prepare a fire in a charcoal grill or preheat a gas grill or oven broiler. Position the grill rack or broiler pan 4–6 inches from the heat source.

Thread the pork onto the skewers and arrange on the grill rack or broiler pan. Grill or broil, turning frequently, until lightly browned, with only a hint of pink in the center, about 3 minutes. Transfer the skewers to a serving platter and garnish with the cilantro and peanuts. Serve hot.

2 tablespoons low-sodium soy sauce

2 tablespoons fresh lime juice

2 tablespoons chopped onion

1 tablespoon creamy natural unsalted peanut butter, stirred well before measuring

1 tablespoon dark honey

1 clove garlic, minced

½ teaspoon ground ginger

¼ teaspoon ground cumin

1 lb pork tenderloin, trimmed of visible fat and cut into ¾-inch cubes

Twelve 12-inch metal or presoaked wooden skewers

1 tablespoon chopped fresh cilantro

2 teaspoons chopped peanuts

NUTRIENT ANALYSIS FOR ONE SERVING

Calories 180	**Carbohydrates** 5 g	**Total Fat** 7 g
Protein 24 g	**Fiber** <1 g	**Saturated Fat** 2 g
Sodium 194 mg	**Sugars** 3 g	**Monounsaturated Fat** 3 g
Cholesterol 71 mg		**Polyunsaturated Fat** 1 g

MUSHROOMS STUFFED WITH TURKEY SAUSAGE

PERCENTAGE OF CALORIES
from total fat   25%
from saturated fat   6%

SERVES 8

Olive oil cooking spray

32 button mushrooms, about 1 lb, brushed clean

6 oz ground turkey breast or chicken breast

½ cup finely chopped sun-dried tomatoes

3 cloves garlic, minced

1 teaspoon chopped fresh basil or ½ teaspoon dried basil

1 teaspoon chopped fresh thyme or ½ teaspoon dried thyme

½ teaspoon fennel seeds

½ teaspoon salt

2 teaspoons olive oil

1 small leek, finely chopped

2 tablespoons grated Parmesan cheese

1 tablespoon chopped fresh parsley

In this version of a popular first-course dish, lean ground turkey is combined with seasonings to make a robust filling with the flavor of Italian sausage. These can be assembled hours ahead and refrigerated, then baked just before serving.

Preheat the oven to 350°F. Spray a shallow baking dish with olive oil cooking spray.

Remove the stems from the mushrooms and set the caps aside. Chop the stems finely. In a large bowl, combine the chopped mushroom stems, ground turkey, sun-dried tomatoes, garlic, basil, thyme, fennel seeds, and salt. Mix well and set aside.

In a nonstick frying pan, heat the olive oil over medium heat. Add the leek and cook, stirring often, until tender, about 4 minutes. Add the turkey breast mixture and cook, stirring often to break up any clumps of meat, until the turkey is opaque throughout, about 4 minutes. Transfer to a bowl.

Add the Parmesan to the bowl with the turkey mixture and stir to combine; the mixture should be just moist enough to stick together slightly. Add a small amount of water if the mixture is too dry.

Heap a mound of about 1 tablespoon filling into each mushroom cap (slightly more or less depending on the size of the mushroom). Arrange the mushrooms in the prepared baking dish. Bake until the mushrooms are tender when pierced with the tip of a knife and the filling is bubbling, about 20 minutes. Garnish with the parsley and serve immediately.

NUTRIENT ANALYSIS FOR ONE SERVING

Calories 71	Carbohydrates 7 g	Total Fat 2 g
Protein 8 g	Fiber 1 g	Saturated Fat <1 g
Sodium 260 mg	Sugars 2 g	Monounsaturated Fat 1 g
Cholesterol 9 mg		Polyunsaturated Fat <1 g

TUNA CROSTINI

PERCENTAGE OF CALORIES
from total fat 31%
from saturated fat 8%

SERVES 6

Crostini are Italian appetizers consisting of thin slices of lightly toasted bread with a flavorful topping that is usually spreadable, like a pâté. If you can't find fresh tuna, you can substitute 9 ounces drained and flaked canned tuna.

Prepare a fire in a charcoal grill or preheat a gas grill or oven broiler. Position the grill rack or broiler pan 4–6 inches from the heat source.

Cut the baguette on the diagonal into 24 slices about ⅓ inch thick. (Reserve any remaining bread for another use.) Set aside.

Lightly brush the tuna with the olive oil. Season with the salt. Grill or broil the tuna, turning once, until opaque throughout and firm to the touch, 8–10 minutes. Transfer to a cutting board and let cool slightly.

Chop the tuna into ¼-inch dice and transfer to a bowl. Add the yogurt, 1 tablespoon of the parsley, the olives, capers, chives, and lemon juice and stir to combine.

Grill the baguette slices, turning once, until lightly toasted, 1–2 minutes. Spoon 1 tablespoon of the tuna mixture onto each toasted baguette slice and top each with a piece or two of red bell pepper and a sprinkle of the remaining 1 tablespoon parsley. Serve immediately.

1 whole-grain baguette, about 10 inches long

12 oz fresh tuna steaks or fillets, about 1 inch thick

1 teaspoon extra-virgin olive oil

⅛ teaspoon salt

3 tablespoons low-fat plain yogurt

2 tablespoons chopped fresh parsley

1 tablespoon chopped pitted Niçoise olives

1 tablespoon capers, drained and chopped

1 tablespoon chopped fresh chives or green onion

2 teaspoons fresh lemon juice

½ red bell pepper, cut into thin strips

NUTRIENT ANALYSIS FOR ONE SERVING

Calories 117	**Carbohydrates** 5 g	**Total Fat** 4 g
Protein 14 g	**Fiber** <1 g	**Saturated Fat** 1 g
Sodium 175 mg	**Sugars** <1 g	**Monounsaturated Fat** 2 g
Cholesterol 22 mg		**Polyunsaturated Fat** 1 g

3g

PERCENTAGE OF CALORIES
from total fat   18%
from saturated fat   4%

BUTTER BEAN SOUP WITH SMOKED TURKEY

SERVES 8

- 1 tablespoon olive oil
- 1 yellow onion, coarsely chopped
- 3 cloves garlic, chopped
- 1 teaspoon chopped fresh thyme or ½ teaspoon dried thyme
- 3 cups fat-free, no-salt-added chicken or vegetable broth, or more as needed
- 1 carrot, peeled and diced
- 3 cups frozen lima beans, thawed
- ½ lb smoked turkey breast, cut into ¼-inch dice
- 1 tablespoon chopped green onion, including tender green parts

Creamy beans with a hint of smokiness make a rich soup. Butter beans are dried large lima beans, named for their city of origin in Peru. You can substitute 1 cup dried beans for the frozen beans. (For tips on cooking dried beans, see page 135.)

In a large saucepan, heat the olive oil over medium-high heat. Add the yellow onion and sauté until soft, about 3 minutes. Add the garlic and thyme and cook for 1 minute; do not let the garlic brown. Add the broth and carrot and bring to a boil. Add the thawed beans and the turkey. Simmer, uncovered, stirring occasionally, until the beans are heated through, about 5 minutes.

Add hot water or additional broth, heated, if the soup is too thick. Ladle into bowls, garnish with the green onion, and serve.

NUTRIENT ANALYSIS FOR ONE SERVING

Calories 147	Carbohydrates 16 g	Total Fat 3 g
Protein 15 g	Fiber 5 g	Saturated Fat <1 g
Sodium 395 mg	Sugars 3 g	Monounsaturated Fat 1 g
Cholesterol 11 mg		Polyunsaturated Fat <1 g

3g

CHICKEN SOUP WITH CARROTS & RICE

PERCENTAGE OF CALORIES

from total fat 16%

from saturated fat 3%

SERVES 6

½ cup brown rice, preferably basmati

¼ teaspoon salt

1 tablespoon olive oil or canola oil

1 yellow onion, diced

1 cup thinly sliced baby carrots

½ celery stalk, diced

1 teaspoon chopped fresh basil or ½ teaspoon dried basil

1 teaspoon chopped fresh thyme or ½ teaspoon dried thyme

½ teaspoon freshly ground pepper

½ bay leaf

4 cups fat-free, no-salt-added chicken broth

¾ lb skinless, boneless chicken breasts, cut into ½-inch pieces

Using brown rice instead of white rice or noodles ups the nutrition value of this famously good-for-you soup. For an Asian flair, add a spoonful of chopped fresh ginger with the onion and use fresh cilantro instead of basil and thyme.

Cook the rice according to the package directions, without added fat but adding the salt to the water.

In a large saucepan, heat the oil over medium-high heat. Add the onion, carrots, and celery and sauté until the vegetables are tender, about 5 minutes. Add the basil, thyme, pepper, bay leaf, and broth and bring to a boil. Cover, reduce the heat to medium-low, and simmer for 5 minutes. Add the chicken and simmer until the chicken is no longer pink throughout, about 3 minutes. Discard the bay leaf. Add the rice and cook for 1 minute longer until the rice is heated through. Serve hot.

NUTRIENT ANALYSIS FOR ONE SERVING

Calories 170	**Carbohydrates** 15 g	**Total Fat** 3 g
Protein 19 g	**Fiber** 2 g	**Saturated Fat** <1 g
Sodium 162 mg	**Sugars** 2 g	**Monounsaturated Fat** 1 g
Cholesterol 33 mg		**Polyunsaturated Fat** <1 g

LENTIL SOUP WITH WATERCRESS

FAT COUNT 2 g

PERCENTAGE OF CALORIES
from total fat   14%
from saturated fat   4%

SERVES 6

Lentils are loaded with protein and fiber, can be kept on hand in the pantry, and cook quickly without presoaking, making lentil soup an excellent anytime meal. Peppery watercress perks up the flavor and adds vibrant color to this earthy soup.

In a large saucepan, heat the oil over medium-high heat. Add the shallot and celery and sauté until the vegetables are tender, about 4 minutes. Add the tomato and oregano and cook for 3 minutes longer. Add the broth and 1 cup water and bring to a boil.

Reduce the heat to medium-low and add the lentils. Return to a simmer and cook for 5 minutes, then add the bulgur. Simmer until the lentils are soft but still intact, about 10 minutes longer. Add more broth if necessary, but the soup should be slightly thickened like a stew.

Remove from the heat and stir in the watercress. Season with the salt and serve immediately.

1 tablespoon olive oil or canola oil

1 shallot, chopped

1 celery stalk, diced

1 tomato, diced

1 teaspoon chopped fresh oregano or ½ teaspoon dried oregano

5 cups fat-free, no-salt-added chicken or vegetable broth, or more as needed

1 cup dried brown lentils, rinsed

⅓ cup medium-grind bulgur

1 cup coarsely chopped watercress leaves

½ teaspoon salt

NUTRIENT ANALYSIS FOR ONE SERVING

Calories 126	**Carbohydrates** 20 g	**Total Fat** 2 g
Protein 12 g	**Fiber** 8 g	**Saturated Fat** <1 g
Sodium 352 mg	**Sugars** 2 g	**Monounsaturated Fat** 2 g
Cholesterol 0 mg		**Polyunsaturated Fat** <1 g

RED BEAN STEW

SERVES 8

FAT COUNT **2**g

PERCENTAGE OF CALORIES
from total fat　　　　　　12%
from saturated fat　　　　3%

This stew is full of texture and rich in flavor. Experiment with different beans, regular or new potatoes, or a variety of fresh herbs. You can substitute 1 cup dried red or pinto beans for the canned beans. (For tips on cooking dried beans, see page 135.)

In a large saucepan, heat the olive oil over medium-high heat. Add the onion and bell pepper and sauté until the onion is soft, about 3 minutes. Add the tomato, garlic, and bay leaf and simmer for 1 minute.

Add the broth and bring to a boil. Add the sweet potato, reduce heat to low, and simmer, uncovered, stirring occasionally, until the sweet potato pieces are tender but still hold their shape, about 5 minutes. Add the beans and cook about 2 minutes longer until just heated through. Discard the bay leaf. Season with the salt and pepper and stir in the cilantro. Serve immediately.

1 tablespoon olive oil

1 yellow onion, coarsely chopped

1 green bell pepper, seeded and diced

1 large tomato, diced

3 cloves garlic, chopped

1 bay leaf

2 cups fat-free, no-salt-added chicken or vegetable broth

1 sweet potato, peeled and diced

3 cups canned red beans (about 2 cans, each 15 oz), rinsed and drained

¼ teaspoon salt

¼ teaspoon freshly ground pepper

2 tablespoons chopped fresh cilantro or parsley

NUTRIENT ANALYSIS FOR ONE SERVING

Calories 149	**Carbohydrates** 25 g	**Total Fat** 2 g
Protein 8 g	**Fiber** 8 g	**Saturated Fat** <1 g
Sodium 297 mg	**Sugars** 6 g	**Monounsaturated Fat** 2 g
Cholesterol 0 mg		**Polyunsaturated Fat** <1 g

4g

ROASTED GARLIC SOUP WITH POTATOES & FENNEL

PERCENTAGE OF CALORIES
from total fat   31%
from saturated fat   4%

SERVES 4

1 fennel bulb, about ½ lb

½ lb new potatoes, peeled and cut into ½-inch cubes

10 cloves garlic

1 tablespoon olive oil

3 cups fat-free, no-salt-added chicken or vegetable broth, or more as needed

1 teaspoon chopped fresh thyme or ½ teaspoon dried thyme

1 teaspoon fresh lemon juice

¼ teaspoon salt

¼ teaspoon freshly ground pepper

Vegetables lightly roasted and then puréed make this a rich and creamy soup. Serve with dark rye bread or crusty whole-grain rolls. If fennel is not available, use 2 celery stalks cut into 1-inch chunks and garnish the soup with chopped fresh parsley.

Preheat the oven to 375°F. Trim the ends and any brown spots off the fennel bulb. Chop a handful of the feathery tops and set aside for garnish. Discard the rest. Cut the fennel bulb through the core into ½-inch slices. Combine the fennel, potatoes, and garlic in a shallow roasting pan. Drizzle with the olive oil and toss to coat. Roast for 10 minutes. Stir the vegetables and continue roasting until lightly golden and nearly tender when pierced with the tip of a knife, about 10 minutes longer.

In a large saucepan, combine the broth and thyme and bring to a boil over high heat. Reduce the heat to low and add the roasted vegetables. Cover and simmer for 5 minutes. Remove from the heat and stir in the lemon juice, salt, and pepper.

Carefully transfer the hot soup in small batches to a blender or food processor. Process until smooth and return each batch to the saucepan. Additional broth can be added if the soup is too thick. Ladle into bowls, garnish with the chopped fennel tops, and serve.

NUTRIENT ANALYSIS FOR ONE SERVING

Calories 118	Carbohydrates 14 g	Total Fat 4 g
Protein 7 g	Fiber 3 g	Saturated Fat <1 g
Sodium 307 mg	Sugars <1 g	Monounsaturated Fat 2 g
Cholesterol 0 mg		Polyunsaturated Fat <1 g

SOUTHWESTERN CHICKEN SOUP

FAT COUNT 4g

PERCENTAGE OF CALORIES
from total fat 18%
from saturated fat 2%

SERVES 6

Robust flavors enliven a soup hearty enough for a main course. This recipe is also a great way to use corn or chicken left over from a barbecue. You can substitute ½ cup dried beans for the canned beans. (For tips on cooking dried beans, see page 135.)

In a large saucepan, heat the olive oil over medium heat. Add the onion and cook slowly until it begins to brown, about 8 minutes.

Add the cumin seeds and sauté until fragrant, about 1 minute.

Add the broth and bring to a simmer. Add the chicken, return to a simmer, and cook until the chicken is opaque throughout, about 3 minutes. Add the black beans, corn, bell pepper, barbecue sauce, and chopped cilantro and cook until heated through, about 3 minutes. Ladle into bowls, garnish with the cilantro sprigs, and serve.

1½ tablespoons olive oil

1 yellow onion, chopped

1 teaspoon cumin seeds

3 cups fat-free, no-salt-added chicken broth

¾ lb skinless, boneless chicken breasts, cut into ½-inch cubes

1½ cups canned black beans (about one 15-oz can), rinsed and drained

1 cup fresh or thawed frozen corn kernels

1 red bell pepper, seeded and diced

¼ cup good-quality barbecue sauce

3 tablespoons chopped fresh cilantro, plus sprigs for garnish

NUTRIENT ANALYSIS FOR ONE SERVING

Calories 196	**Carbohydrates** 20 g	**Total Fat** 4 g
Protein 21 g	**Fiber** 5 g	**Saturated Fat** <1 g
Sodium 295 mg	**Sugars** 5 g	**Monounsaturated Fat** 2 g
Cholesterol 33 mg		**Polyunsaturated Fat** <1 g

TOMATO & SPINACH SOUP

SERVES 6

1 tablespoon olive oil or canola oil

1 yellow onion, chopped

2 lb plum (Roma) tomatoes, chopped

2 tablespoons minced fresh basil

2 cups fat-free, no-salt-added chicken or vegetable broth

1 cup chopped fresh spinach

½ teaspoon salt

¼ teaspoon freshly ground pepper

2 tablespoons grated Parmesan cheese

A quick simmer of a few fresh ingredients yields a rich, vibrant soup that takes minutes to prepare. In place of spinach, try kale, chard, or watercress.

In a large saucepan, heat the oil over medium-high heat. Add the onion and sauté until soft, about 4 minutes. Add the tomatoes and basil and cook until the tomatoes are tender, about 5 minutes.

Carefully transfer the tomato mixture to a blender or food processor. Process until puréed and return to the saucepan. Add the broth and bring to a boil.

Add the chopped spinach and cook until the spinach is just wilted, about 1 minute. Season with the salt and pepper. Ladle into bowls, garnish with the Parmesan, and serve immediately.

NUTRIENT ANALYSIS FOR ONE SERVING

Calories 78	Carbohydrates 9 g	Total Fat 3 g
Protein 4 g	Fiber 2 g	Saturated Fat <1 g
Sodium 301 mg	Sugars 5 g	Monounsaturated Fat 2 g
Cholesterol 1 mg		Polyunsaturated Fat <1 g

BRUSSELS SPROUTS & APPLE SALAD

FAT COUNT 3g

PERCENTAGE OF CALORIES
from total fat | 25%
from saturated fat | 4%

SERVES 4

Brussels sprouts are in prime form when the heads are hard and the leaves tightly bunched. If you can't find them fresh, thawed frozen sprouts work well in this tangy, crunchy salad.

Put the walnuts in a small, dry frying pan over medium-high heat. Cook, stirring often, until fragrant and lightly toasted, 3–5 minutes. Immediately transfer to a plate to cool and set aside.

In a large bowl, whisk together the yogurt, maple syrup, salt, pepper, and 1 teaspoon of the lemon juice. In a small bowl, toss the apple slices with the remaining 1 teaspoon lemon juice and stir into the yogurt mixture. Set aside.

In a saucepan fitted with a steamer basket, bring 1 inch of water to a boil. Add the brussels sprouts and steam until tender-crisp, about 4 minutes. Let cool slightly.

Add the brussels sprouts to the bowl with the yogurt mixture and apples and toss gently to coat.

Divide the salad among individual plates and sprinkle with the lemon zest and toasted walnuts. Serve immediately.

2 tablespoons chopped walnuts

½ cup nonfat plain yogurt

1½ teaspoons maple syrup

¼ teaspoon salt

⅛ teaspoon freshly ground pepper

2 teaspoons fresh lemon juice

1 apple, halved, cored, and thinly sliced

½ lb brussels sprouts, trimmed and quartered

1 teaspoon grated lemon zest

NUTRIENT ANALYSIS FOR ONE SERVING

Calories 109	Carbohydrates 19 g	Total Fat 3 g
Protein 6 g	Fiber 3 g	Saturated Fat <1 g
Sodium 171 mg	Sugars 9 g	Monounsaturated Fat <1 g
Cholesterol <1 mg		Polyunsaturated Fat 1 g

CABBAGE SALAD WITH MANGO & PEANUTS

SERVES 6

½ head green cabbage, trimmed, cored, and thinly sliced (about 6 cups)

2½ cups peeled and diced mango (page 137)

1 celery stalk, halved lengthwise and sliced thinly on the diagonal

1 large carrot, peeled and grated

2 green onions, including tender green parts, chopped

¼ cup creamy natural unsalted peanut butter, stirred well before measuring

2 tablespoons fresh lime juice

2 tablespoons low-sodium soy sauce

2 tablespoons chopped fresh cilantro

2 cloves garlic, finely chopped

½ teaspoon ground ginger

2 teaspoons chopped unsalted dry-roasted peanuts

The creamy, garlicky dressing for this fiber-rich salad is reminiscent of Thai peanut sauce. For a milder-flavored salad, try savoy or napa cabbage.

In a large bowl, combine the cabbage, mango, celery, carrot, and green onions and toss to mix.

In a blender or food processor, combine the peanut butter, lime juice, soy sauce, cilantro, garlic, ginger, and 2 tablespoons water. Process until smooth and the consistency of thick cream. If the dressing is too thick, add 1–2 tablespoons additional water.

Pour the dressing over the vegetables and toss well. Garnish with the chopped peanuts and serve.

NUTRIENT ANALYSIS FOR ONE SERVING

Calories 152	**Carbohydrates** 23 g	**Total Fat** 6 g
Protein 5 g	**Fiber** 5 g	**Saturated Fat** 1 g
Sodium 209 mg	**Sugars** 15 g	**Monounsaturated Fat** 3 g
Cholesterol 0 mg		**Polyunsaturated Fat** 2 g

GRAPEFRUIT & AVOCADO WITH CILANTRO CREAM

FAT COUNT 2 g

PERCENTAGE OF CALORIES
from total fat 33%
from saturated fat 7%

SERVES 6

Juicy grapefruit and creamy avocado blend together in this salad with a zippy yogurt dressing. If you can't find baby lettuces, tender baby spinach leaves are the perfect substitute.

In a small bowl, whisk together the yogurt, cilantro, lime juice, honey, grapefruit zest, and salt. Set aside.

Peel and cut the avocado half lengthwise into 6 slices.

Cut a slice off the top and bottom of the grapefruit, then stand it upright. Following the contour of the fruit, slice off the peel and white pith in thick strips. Holding the fruit over a bowl, cut along each side of the membranes between the sections, letting the freed section and any juices drop into the bowl. Cut any large sections in half crosswise.

Divide the lettuce among individual plates. Arrange the grapefruit pieces and avocado slices on each plate and drizzle about 2 tablespoons of the cilantro cream over each salad. Serve immediately.

½ cup low-fat plain yogurt

2 tablespoons finely chopped fresh cilantro

1 tablespoon fresh lime juice

1 teaspoon dark honey

1 teaspoon grated grapefruit zest

¼ teaspoon salt

½ medium-firm ripe avocado, pitted

1 large pink grapefruit

6 cups baby lettuce leaves

NUTRIENT ANALYSIS FOR ONE SERVING

Calories 55	Carbohydrates 7 g	Total Fat 2 g
Protein 2 g	Fiber 3 g	Saturated Fat <1 g
Sodium 118 mg	Sugars 4 g	Monounsaturated Fat <1 g
Cholesterol <1 mg		Polyunsaturated Fat <1 g

TOMATOES WITH CUCUMBERS & YOGURT

PERCENTAGE OF CALORIES

from total fat 23%

from saturated fat 7%

SERVES 4

1 cucumber, peeled, seeded, and diced

2 plum (Roma) tomatoes, seeded (see note at right) and diced

1 green onion, including tender green parts, minced

2 tablespoons finely chopped fresh mint

2 tablespoons finely chopped fresh parsley

1 clove garlic, finely chopped

1 cup low-fat plain yogurt

¼ teaspoon salt

¼ teaspoon freshly ground pepper

To seed tomatoes, cut them in half crosswise, hold each half over a bowl, and squeeze and shake gently to dislodge the seeds. This light salad is similar to Indian raita, a dish served with curries. It goes well with grilled chicken or a sandwich.

In a bowl, combine the cucumber, tomatoes, green onion, mint, parsley, garlic, yogurt, salt, and pepper. Refrigerate for at least 1 hour to allow the flavors to blend. Serve chilled or at room temperature.

NUTRIENT ANALYSIS FOR ONE SERVING

Calories 39	**Carbohydrates** 7 g	**Total Fat** <1 g
Protein 3 g	**Fiber** 1 g	**Saturated Fat** <1 g
Sodium 178 mg	**Sugars** 4 g	**Monounsaturated Fat** <1 g
Cholesterol 2 mg		**Polyunsaturated Fat** <1 g

1 g

MARINATED CORN SALAD

SERVES 4

1 teaspoon olive oil

1 yellow onion, chopped

1 green bell pepper, chopped

1 large tomato, chopped

1 zucchini, halved lengthwise and thinly sliced crosswise

2 cups fresh or thawed frozen corn kernels

3 cloves garlic, finely chopped

½ teaspoon ground cumin

½ teaspoon salt

2 tablespoons balsamic or red wine vinegar

1 tablespoon chopped fresh parsley or cilantro

A multicolored dish that will brighten any table or picnic basket, this fresh salad stands well on its own but also adds a complementary zing to a meal of chicken fajitas or burritos.

In a large nonstick frying pan, heat the olive oil over medium-high heat. Add the onion and bell pepper and sauté until soft, about 4 minutes. Add the tomato, zucchini, corn, garlic, cumin, and salt and sauté until the vegetables are tender-crisp, about 5 minutes longer. Transfer to a bowl and let cool slightly.

Add the vinegar to the vegetables and toss to combine. Garnish with the parsley and serve.

NUTRIENT ANALYSIS FOR ONE SERVING

Calories 51	**Carbohydrates** 9 g	**Total Fat** 1 g
Protein 2 g	**Fiber** 2 g	**Saturated Fat** <1 g
Sodium 305 mg	**Sugars** 5 g	**Monounsaturated Fat** 1 g
Cholesterol 0 mg		**Polyunsaturated Fat** <1 g

WHITE BEAN & BULGUR SALAD

FAT COUNT 2g

PERCENTAGE OF CALORIES
from total fat 14%
from saturated fat 3%

SERVES 8

This easy fiber-rich salad lends itself to variations. In place of the white beans, parsley, and lemon juice, try using black beans, cilantro, and lime juice. It's great as a side dish or tucked into a pita-bread sandwich.

Combine the bulgur with the hot broth in a large bowl. Cover and let stand for 30 minutes. When the bulgur has cooled to room temperature, add the lemon juice, parsley, tomato, olive oil, salt, and pepper and stir to combine.

Add the beans to the bowl with the bulgur mixture, toss to combine, and serve immediately.

1 cup coarse-grind bulgur

2 cups fat-free, no-salt-added chicken or vegetable broth, heated

2 tablespoons fresh lemon juice

2 tablespoons chopped fresh parsley

1 large tomato, chopped

1 tablespoon extra-virgin olive oil

½ teaspoon salt

¼ teaspoon freshly ground pepper

1½ cups canned Great Northern or other white beans (about one 15-oz can), drained and rinsed

NUTRIENT ANALYSIS FOR ONE SERVING

Calories 131	**Carbohydrates** 24 g	**Total Fat** 2 g
Protein 6 g	**Fiber** 6 g	**Saturated Fat** <1 g
Sodium 187 mg	**Sugars** 3 g	**Monounsaturated Fat** 1 g
Cholesterol 0 mg		**Polyunsaturated Fat** <1 g

SUMMER MELON SALAD

FAT COUNT

1 g

PERCENTAGE OF CALORIES
from total fat   8%
from saturated fat   4%

SERVES 8

This flavorful medley of watermelon and cantaloupe is perfect for breakfast, as a snack, or for dessert. The tangy, minty syrup can be prepared a day ahead.

In a small saucepan, combine the honey, lemon juice, and zest. Bring to a boil over medium heat, stirring occasionally. Reduce the heat to low and simmer until the mixture is reduced by half, about 5 minutes. Remove from the heat and let cool to room temperature.

In a large bowl, combine the watermelon and cantaloupe. Divide the melon mixture among individual serving bowls. Drizzle the cooled syrup over each serving and garnish with the almonds and mint.

¼ cup dark honey

⅓ cup fresh lemon juice

1 teaspoon grated lemon zest

2 lb seedless watermelon, rind removed, diced (about 5 cups)

One 6-inch firm, ripe cantaloupe (about 3 lb), rind removed, seeded, and diced (about 5 cups)

2 tablespoons slivered almonds, lightly toasted (page 138)

2 tablespoons fresh mint, cut into thin strips

NUTRIENT ANALYSIS FOR ONE SERVING

Calories 108	**Carbohydrates** 25 g	**Total Fat** 1 g
Protein 2 g	**Fiber** 2 g	**Saturated Fat** <1 g
Sodium 11 mg	**Sugars** 22 g	**Monounsaturated Fat** <1 g
Cholesterol 0 mg		**Polyunsaturated Fat** <1 g

MAIN DISHES

Pasta with Grilled Tomatoes & Feta, 93

BAKED HALIBUT WITH FRESH CITRUS

SERVES 4

Olive oil cooking spray

1 tablespoon olive oil

¼ cup grated onion

¾ cup fresh orange juice

1 tomato, seeded (page 54) and chopped

1 teaspoon dark honey

1 teaspoon chopped fresh thyme or ½ teaspoon dried thyme

4 halibut fillets, each about 5 oz and 1 inch thick

½ teaspoon salt

¼ teaspoon freshly ground pepper

1 tablespoon chopped fresh parsley

1 teaspoon grated orange zest

This easy dish is delicious when served with whole-wheat couscous or brown rice. If you can't find halibut, another firm-fleshed fish such as cod or swordfish will also make this a tender, heart-healthy dish.

Preheat the oven to 375°F. Select a shallow baking dish just large enough to hold the halibut fillets in a single layer and lightly coat the dish with olive oil cooking spray.

In a sauté pan, heat the olive oil over medium heat. Add the onion and sauté until it is just golden, about 4 minutes. Add the orange juice, tomato, honey, and thyme and cook, stirring occasionally, until thickened, 3–5 minutes longer. Remove from the heat and let the sauce cool for about 10 minutes.

Spoon half of the sauce into the prepared baking dish. Arrange the fillets on top of the sauce and sprinkle with the salt and pepper. Spoon the remaining sauce over the fish and cover the dish with aluminum foil. Bake until the fillets are opaque throughout when tested with the tip of a knife, about 12 minutes.

Place the fillets on warmed individual plates and cover to keep warm. Pour the pan juices from the baking dish into the sauté pan and bring to a boil over medium heat. Cook until the sauce is reduced and the juices are thickened, about 2 minutes. Spoon the sauce over the fish and garnish with the parsley and orange zest. Serve immediately.

NUTRIENT ANALYSIS FOR ONE SERVING

Calories 235	**Carbohydrates** 12 g	**Total Fat** 7 g
Protein 30 g	**Fiber** 1 g	**Saturated Fat** 1 g
Sodium 228 mg	**Sugars** 11 g	**Monounsaturated Fat** 4 g
Cholesterol 45 mg		**Polyunsaturated Fat** 1 g

GRILLED SHRIMP SALAD

PERCENTAGE OF CALORIES
from total fat — 35%
from saturated fat — 4%

SERVES 4

The ingredients for this salad—even the grilled shrimp—can be prepared in advance. Just keep everything chilled and assemble right before serving. Cantaloupe, rich in vitamin A, makes a fine substitute for the papaya.

Prepare a fire in a charcoal grill or preheat a gas grill or oven broiler. Away from the heat source, lightly coat the grill rack or broiler pan with olive oil cooking spray. Position the grill rack or broiler pan 4–6 inches from the heat source.

In a small bowl, whisk together the olive oil, lemon juice, green onion, red pepper flakes (if using), ⅛ teaspoon of the salt, and the white pepper. Set the dressing aside.

Arrange the shrimp on the grill rack or broiler pan. Season with the remaining ⅛ teaspoon salt. Grill or broil until opaque, about 1½ minutes on each side. Cover and keep warm.

In a large bowl, combine the spinach, cucumber, papaya, tomatoes, bell pepper, basil, and cilantro. Add the dressing and toss to coat. Divide the salad among chilled individual plates. Divide the shrimp among the salads, arranging them around the edges. Serve immediately.

Olive oil cooking spray

5 teaspoons extra-virgin olive oil

2 tablespoons fresh lemon juice

1 tablespoon minced green onion

½ teaspoon red pepper flakes (optional)

¼ teaspoon salt

¼ teaspoon ground white pepper

1 lb large shrimp (prawns), peeled and deveined, tails intact

4 cups shredded spinach

1 cucumber, peeled, seeded, and diced

1 small papaya, seeded and cut into ½-inch cubes

½ cup cherry tomatoes, halved

½ yellow bell pepper, cut into thin strips

1 tablespoon chopped fresh basil

1 tablespoon chopped fresh cilantro

NUTRIENT ANALYSIS FOR ONE SERVING

Calories 207	**Carbohydrates** 10 g	**Total Fat** 8 g
Protein 25 g	**Fiber** 2 g	**Saturated Fat** 1 g
Sodium 338 mg	**Sugars** 3 g	**Monounsaturated Fat** 4 g
Cholesterol 172 mg		**Polyunsaturated Fat** 1 g

FAT COUNT

7 g

PERCENTAGE OF CALORIES
from total fat   27%
from saturated fat   4%

SALMON WITH TOASTED BULGUR, LIME & GINGER

SERVES 4

1 teaspoon ground coriander

1 teaspoon ground cumin

1 teaspoon curry powder

4 salmon fillets, about 5 oz each

Olive oil cooking spray

For the lime dressing:

2 tablespoons rice wine vinegar

2 tablespoons fresh lime juice

1 tablespoon low-sodium
soy sauce

1 tablespoon chopped fresh
cilantro

2 teaspoons Dijon mustard

2 teaspoons peeled, finely chopped
fresh ginger

For the bulgur:

2 teaspoons olive oil

1½ teaspoons mustard seeds

½ yellow onion, finely chopped

¼ cup *each* finely diced red bell
pepper and yellow bell pepper

1 cup coarse-grind bulgur

2 cups fat-free, no-salt-added
chicken broth

¼ teaspoon *each* salt and freshly
ground black pepper

½ teaspoon red pepper flakes

3 tablespoons finely chopped fresh
cilantro, plus sprigs for garnish

Get a good dose of heart-healthy omega-3 fatty acids from the salmon in this flavorful and well-balanced dish. Serve with a crisp stir-fry of bok choy or leafy green vegetables.

In a small bowl, stir together the coriander, cumin, and curry powder. Place the salmon fillets on a plate. Sprinkle ½ teaspoon of the spice mixture over each fillet. Cover with plastic wrap and refrigerate for 2–3 hours.

To make the dressing, in a small bowl, whisk together the vinegar, lime juice, soy sauce, cilantro, mustard, ginger, and 1 tablespoon water. Set aside.

To make the bulgur, heat the olive oil in a nonstick saucepan over medium heat. Add the mustard seeds, onion, and bell peppers and sauté for about 1 minute. Add the bulgur and stir frequently until the bulgur is lightly toasted, about 3 minutes. Remove from the heat and carefully stir in the broth. Return the pan to medium heat and bring to a boil. Reduce the heat to low, cover, and simmer until almost all of the broth is absorbed, about 12 minutes. Season with the salt and black pepper. Stir in the red pepper flakes and the chopped cilantro. Set aside and keep warm.

Meanwhile, away from the heat source, lightly coat a large nonstick sauté pan with olive oil cooking spray. Heat the pan over medium-high heat and add the salmon fillets, flesh side down. Sear until browned and crisp, about 3 minutes. Turn the fillets and cook until opaque throughout when tested with the tip of a knife, about 3 minutes longer. Divide the bulgur among individual plates. Top each serving with a salmon fillet. Drizzle with the dressing and garnish with the cilantro sprigs. Serve immediately.

NUTRIENT ANALYSIS FOR ONE SERVING

Calories 235	**Carbohydrates** 22 g	**Total Fat** 7 g
Protein 21 g	**Fiber** 5 g	**Saturated Fat** 1 g
Sodium 325 mg	**Sugars** 1 g	**Monounsaturated Fat** 3 g
Cholesterol 42 mg		**Polyunsaturated Fat** 2 g

MUSTARD-BRAISED COD WITH WILTED CHARD

SERVES 4

- 1 tablespoon olive oil
- 2 tablespoons finely chopped onion
- 2 tablespoons finely chopped carrot
- 2 tablespoons finely chopped celery
- ½ cup fish stock, bottled clam juice, or fat-free, no-salt-added chicken broth
- ½ cup dry white wine
- 1¼ lb fresh cod fillets
- 4 cups thinly shredded Swiss chard
- 1 teaspoon Dijon mustard
- 1 teaspoon fresh lemon juice
- 1 tablespoon chopped fresh parsley
- ½ teaspoon salt
- ¼ teaspoon freshly ground pepper

The tang of fresh lemon juice and mustard brings out the mild flavors of cod. If Swiss chard isn't available, try spinach or other cooking greens. If you prefer not to use wine, omit the white wine in this recipe and increase the fish stock to 1 cup.

In a sauté pan large enough to hold the cod fillets in a single layer without crowding, heat the olive oil over medium heat. Add the onion, carrot, and celery and sauté until the vegetables are softened, about 3 minutes. Add the stock and the wine and bring to a boil. Reduce the heat to low and add the fillets to the pan. Return to a simmer, cover, and simmer slowly until the fish is opaque throughout when tested with the tip of a knife, about 5 minutes, depending on the thickness of the fillets. Carefully remove the fish with a slotted spatula and transfer to warmed individual plates. Cover to keep warm.

Add the shredded chard to the pan with the juices, cover, and cook over medium heat just until wilted, about 2 minutes. Divide the chard among the plates.

Bring the pan juices to a boil and whisk in the mustard, lemon juice, parsley, salt, and pepper. Spoon over the fillets and serve immediately.

NUTRIENT ANALYSIS FOR ONE SERVING

Calories 183	Carbohydrates 3 g	Total Fat 5 g
Protein 23 g	Fiber 1 g	Saturated Fat 1 g
Sodium 360 mg	Sugars 1 g	Monounsaturated Fat 3 g
Cholesterol 61 mg		Polyunsaturated Fat 1 g

TUNA STEAKS WITH SOY-MUSTARD VINAIGRETTE

PERCENTAGE OF CALORIES
from total fat 25%
from saturated fat 4%

SERVES 4

This savory dish takes just minutes to prepare and is especially good for your heart. Watch the tuna carefully as it sears in the pan—it's easy to overcook.

In a small bowl, whisk together the broth, vinegar, soy sauce, lemon juice, orange juice, mustard, and ginger. Set aside.

In another small bowl, combine the oils. Brush over the tuna steaks and sprinkle with the salt and pepper. Heat a large nonstick frying pan over medium-high heat. Add the tuna and sear, turning once, until browned on the outside but still rare on the inside, about 3 minutes on each side, or longer for more well done tuna. Transfer the tuna to a platter, cover, and keep warm.

Add the spinach to the hot pan and cook, stirring constantly, just until wilted, about 2 minutes. Divide among warmed individual plates and place a tuna steak on top of each portion. Keep warm.

Add the vinaigrette mixture to the hot pan and cook just until it comes to a boil. Pour over the tuna steaks and garnish with the chives. Serve immediately.

¼ cup fat-free, no-salt-added chicken broth

1 tablespoon rice wine vinegar

1 tablespoon low-sodium soy sauce

1 tablespoon fresh lemon juice

1 tablespoon fresh orange juice

½ teaspoon dry mustard

½ teaspoon ground ginger

1 tablespoon olive oil

1 teaspoon sesame oil

4 tuna steaks, each about 5 oz and 1 inch thick

¼ teaspoon salt

¼ teaspoon freshly ground pepper

4 cups baby spinach leaves or other baby greens

1 tablespoon chopped fresh chives or green onion

NUTRIENT ANALYSIS FOR ONE SERVING

Calories 214	**Carbohydrates** 3 g	**Total Fat** 6 g
Protein 36 g	**Fiber** 2 g	**Saturated Fat** 1 g
Sodium 242 mg	**Sugars** <1 g	**Monounsaturated Fat** 3 g
Cholesterol 64 mg		**Polyunsaturated Fat** 1 g

SWORDFISH KABOBS

FAT COUNT

8g

PERCENTAGE OF CALORIES

from total fat   30%
from saturated fat   4%

SERVES 4

The easy marinade for the swordfish is also good on halibut and tuna. For perfect even cooking, cut the fish into pieces of uniform size. If using wooden skewers, soak them in water for about 30 minutes before grilling or broiling to prevent burning.

In a blender or food processor, combine the olive oil, lemon juice, onion, parsley, paprika, bay leaf, pepper, and 2 tablespoons water. Process until puréed. Pour into a shallow baking dish. Add the swordfish and toss to coat. Cover and marinate at room temperature for 30 minutes or in the refrigerator for up to 2 hours.

Remove the swordfish from the marinade and discard the marinade. Drain and blot dry to remove excess marinade.

Prepare a fire in a charcoal grill or preheat a gas grill or oven broiler. Away from the heat source, lightly spray the grill rack or broiler pan with olive oil cooking spray. Position the grill rack or broiler pan 4–6 inches from the heat source.

Thread the fish and the bell pepper, tomato, and onion pieces onto the skewers in alternating layers. Arrange the kabobs on the grill rack or broiler pan and season with the salt. Grill or broil, turning every 2 minutes, until the swordfish is opaque throughout when tested with the tip of a knife, 5–6 minutes. Serve immediately.

1 tablespoon extra-virgin olive oil

1 tablespoon fresh lemon juice

2 tablespoons chopped onion

2 tablespoons chopped fresh parsley

½ teaspoon paprika

½ bay leaf

⅛ teaspoon freshly ground pepper

1¼ lb swordfish fillets, cut into 1-inch cubes

Olive oil cooking spray

1 green bell pepper, cut into 1-inch pieces

1 yellow bell pepper, cut into 1-inch pieces

4 plum (Roma) tomatoes, cut into 1-inch pieces

1 red onion, cut into 1-inch pieces

Four 12-inch metal or presoaked wooden skewers

½ teaspoon salt

NUTRIENT ANALYSIS FOR ONE SERVING

Calories 239	**Carbohydrates** 9 g	**Total Fat** 8 g
Protein 28 g	**Fiber** 2 g	**Saturated Fat** 1 g
Sodium 394 mg	**Sugars** 4 g	**Monounsaturated Fat** 5 g
Cholesterol 52 mg		**Polyunsaturated Fat** 1 g

FAT COUNT

7 g

BAKED CHICKEN WITH APRICOT COMPOTE

PERCENTAGE OF CALORIES

from total fat   27%

from saturated fat   4%

SERVES 4

1 tablespoon olive oil

2 yellow onions, peeled, halved vertically, and thinly sliced crosswise

¼ teaspoon ground coriander

⅛ teaspoon ground ginger

⅛ teaspoon ground cumin

½ cup fat-free, no-salt-added chicken broth

4 apricots, pitted and quartered, or ½ cup dried apricots, slivered

2 tablespoons chopped fresh cilantro, plus sprigs for garnish

4 skinless, boneless chicken breasts, about 4 oz each

½ teaspoon salt

¼ teaspoon ground white pepper

2 tablespoons chopped walnuts or almonds, toasted (page 138)

Parchment packets make nice servings of juicy chicken topped with antioxidant-rich fruit. The packets can be assembled a few hours ahead of time and baked just before dinner. Aluminum foil can be used in place of parchment paper.

In a sauté pan, heat the olive oil over medium-high heat. Add the onions, coriander, ginger, and cumin. Cook until the onions are softened and just starting to brown, about 6 minutes. Add the broth and apricots, bring to a simmer, and cook until the apricots are soft and the juices are reduced, about 3 minutes. Sprinkle the chopped cilantro over the apricots and set the mixture aside to cool.

Preheat the oven to 375°F. Cut out four 12-inch squares of parchment paper. Fold a square in half to create a crease, then open it up. Place a chicken breast on one side of the crease. Repeat with the remaining breasts and squares of paper. Sprinkle each with the salt and white pepper. Top each chicken breast with one-fourth of the apricot compote. Sprinkle each with one-fourth of the nuts.

Fold the paper squares in half over the chicken breasts, and then tightly fold in the edges, crimping around all sides to seal the packets completely. Place the packets on a baking sheet.

Bake until the parchment packets are lightly browned and puffy, about 10 minutes. Transfer the packets to warmed individual plates. To serve, slit each packet with an X and fold back the paper. Garnish with the cilantro sprigs and serve immediately.

NUTRIENT ANALYSIS FOR ONE SERVING

Calories 231	**Carbohydrates** 14 g	**Total Fat** 7 g
Protein 29 g	**Fiber** 3 g	**Saturated Fat** 1 g
Sodium 380 mg	**Sugars** 8 g	**Monounsaturated Fat** 3 g
Cholesterol 44 mg		**Polyunsaturated Fat** 2 g

CHICKEN & VEGETABLE STEW

SERVES 6

Ingredients

- 10 oz baby onions or 1 cup thawed frozen pearl onions
- 1 tablespoon olive oil
- 1 celery stalk, diced
- 10 baby carrots, halved and thinly sliced crosswise
- 1 red bell pepper, seeded and diced
- 1 tomato, seeded (page 54) and diced
- 4 cups fat-free, no-salt-added chicken broth
- 1½ cups canned pinto beans or white soybeans (about three-fourths of a 15-oz can), rinsed and drained
- 1 sweet potato, peeled and diced
- 1 lb skinless, boneless chicken breasts, cut into 1-inch cubes
- 1 cup shelled English peas or fresh soybeans (edamame)
- 2 cups chopped Swiss chard or spinach
- 2 teaspoons chopped fresh dill or ½ teaspoon dried dill
- 2 teaspoons chopped fresh basil or ½ teaspoon dried basil
- 1 teaspoon salt
- ½ teaspoon freshly ground pepper

Full of colorful vegetables and thickened with nutritious pinto beans, this delicious stew is a complete meal in itself. A crisp green salad is the perfect complement.

Bring a saucepan three-fourths full of water to a boil, add the baby onions, and let stand (blanch) for 1 minute. Drain and immerse the onions in cold water for 5 minutes to stop the cooking. Drain again and slip off the skins. Using a small, sharp knife, trim away the root and stem ends. Set aside.

In a large, heavy saucepan, heat the olive oil over medium heat. Add the celery, carrots, and onions; reduce the heat to a gentle simmer and cook until the vegetables are softened, about 5 minutes. Add the bell pepper and tomato and cook for 3 minutes longer.

Add 3 cups of the broth and bring to a simmer. Meanwhile, combine the remaining 1 cup broth and the beans in a food processor. Process until puréed; add the purée to the pan.

Add the sweet potato and chicken to the pan, return to a simmer, and cook until the chicken is opaque throughout, about 4 minutes. Stir in the peas, Swiss chard, dill, basil, salt, and pepper. Cover and cook until the peas are heated through and the chard is wilted, about 1 minute. Serve hot.

NUTRIENT ANALYSIS FOR ONE SERVING

Calories 275	Carbohydrates 30 g	Total Fat 6 g
Protein 26 g	Fiber 6 g	Saturated Fat 1 g
Sodium 285 mg	Sugars 6 g	Monounsaturated Fat 4 g
Cholesterol 44 mg		Polyunsaturated Fat <1 g

CHICKEN WITH ROSEMARY & PEARL ONIONS

SERVES 4

Serve this fragrant chicken dish with nutrient-dense broccoli and creamy polenta or roasted potatoes. Turkey breast can be substituted with the same delicious results.

Bring a saucepan three-fourths full of water to a boil, add the pearl onions, and let stand (blanch) for 1 minute. Drain and immerse in cold water for 5 minutes to stop the cooking. Drain again and slip off the skins. Using a small, sharp knife, trim away the root and stem ends. Set aside.

In another saucepan, heat the olive oil over medium heat. Add the tomato and garlic and cook for about 2 minutes. Sprinkle with the flour and whisk for about 1 minute. Add the broth in a stream, continuing to whisk to keep lumps from forming. Reduce the heat to low and whisk in the chopped rosemary, salt, pepper, and nutmeg. Bring to a boil over high heat, stirring constantly until thickened. Reduce the heat to low and add the pearl onions and the chicken. Simmer until the chicken is opaque throughout, about 4 minutes. Serve immediately, garnished with the rosemary sprigs.

10 oz pearl onions

2 tablespoons olive oil

1 tomato, peeled, seeded (page 54), and finely chopped

1 clove garlic, minced

2 tablespoons all-purpose flour

1½ cups fat-free, no-salt-added chicken broth

½ teaspoon finely chopped fresh rosemary, plus sprigs for garnish

¾ teaspoon salt

¼ teaspoon freshly ground pepper

Pinch of ground nutmeg

1 lb skinless, boneless chicken breasts, cut into thin strips

NUTRIENT ANALYSIS FOR ONE SERVING

Calories 242	**Carbohydrates** 17 g	**Total Fat** 8 g
Protein 30 g	**Fiber** 2 g	**Saturated Fat** 1 g
Sodium 374 mg	**Sugars** 5 g	**Monounsaturated Fat** 5 g
Cholesterol 66 mg		**Polyunsaturated Fat** 1 g

PERCENTAGE OF CALORIES
from total fat   20%
from saturated fat   3%

TURKEY PITA SANDWICHES

SERVES 8

¼ cup silken tofu

2 tablespoons Dijon mustard

2 tablespoons tahini

1 tablespoon fresh lemon juice

½ teaspoon olive oil

1 lb ground turkey

¼ cup chopped fresh cilantro

¼ cup chopped fresh mint

3 cloves garlic, minced

¼ teaspoon red pepper flakes
   (optional)

¼ teaspoon salt

¼ teaspoon freshly ground
   black pepper

Four 6-inch whole-wheat pita
   breads, halved crosswise

2½ cups shredded romaine lettuce

8 large tomato slices

In this flavorful dish, lean seasoned turkey is tucked into warm pita pockets. Serve with Tomatoes with Cucumbers & Yogurt (page 54) and White Bean & Bulgur Salad (page 57).

In a blender, combine the tofu, mustard, tahini, and lemon juice and blend until smooth. Transfer the sauce to a bowl and set aside.

In another bowl, combine the olive oil, turkey, cilantro, mint, garlic, red pepper flakes (if using), salt, and black pepper. Heat a large nonstick frying pan over medium heat. Add the turkey mixture and sauté, stirring often to break up any clumps of meat, until the turkey is lightly browned and cooked through, about 4 minutes. Set aside and keep warm.

Warm the pita halves in a toaster or in the oven on a low setting. Spread a heaping tablespoon of sauce inside each pocket. Divide the lettuce and tomatoes among the pita pockets. Stuff each with the turkey mixture. Serve immediately.

NUTRIENT ANALYSIS FOR ONE SERVING

Calories 194	**Carbohydrates** 22 g	**Total Fat** 7 g
Protein 14 g	**Fiber** 4 g	**Saturated Fat** 1 g
Sodium 377 mg	**Sugars** 2 g	**Monounsaturated Fat** 2 g
Cholesterol 30 mg		**Polyunsaturated Fat** 2 g

GRILLED JERK TURKEY BREAST

FAT COUNT

8g

PERCENTAGE OF CALORIES

| from total fat | 34% |
| from saturated fat | 4% |

SERVES 4

Thin slices of turkey cook quickly and are great for sandwiches. The jerk marinade works well with chicken and lean meats, too. To heighten the spiciness, add more cayenne.

In a shallow baking dish, combine the paprika, ginger, thyme, black pepper, allspice, cayenne (if using), and nutmeg. Add the soy sauce, olive oil, 2 tablespoons water, the honey, and the garlic. Stir well to combine.

Place the turkey breast on a cutting board and carve into 8 thin slices. Lay the turkey slices flat and cover with plastic wrap. With a kitchen mallet, pound the slices gently to flatten. Place in the marinade and turn once to coat. Marinate, covered and refrigerated, for 3–4 hours or up to 6 hours.

Prepare a fire in a charcoal grill or preheat a gas grill or oven broiler. Position the grill rack or broiler pan 4–6 inches from the heat source.

Remove the turkey from the marinade and arrange on the grill rack or broiler pan. Discard the marinade. Grill or broil the turkey slices until opaque throughout, about 1 minute on each side. Watch carefully to prevent burning. Serve immediately.

½ teaspoon paprika

½ teaspoon ground ginger

½ teaspoon dried thyme

¼ teaspoon freshly ground black pepper

¼ teaspoon ground allspice

⅛ teaspoon cayenne pepper (optional)

Pinch of ground nutmeg

2 tablespoons low-sodium soy sauce

2 tablespoons olive oil

1 tablespoon dark honey

1 clove garlic, minced

1 lb skinless, boneless turkey breast

NUTRIENT ANALYSIS FOR ONE SERVING

Calories 210	Carbohydrates 6 g	Total Fat 8 g
Protein 28 g	Fiber <1 g	Saturated Fat 1 g
Sodium 333 mg	Sugars 4 g	Monounsaturated Fat 5 g
Cholesterol 70 mg		Polyunsaturated Fat <1 g

GRILLED STEAK WITH MUSHROOMS & TOMATOES

3g

PERCENTAGE OF CALORIES
from total fat   14%
from saturated fat   5%

SERVES 4

There's no better way to bring out the best in a lean cut of meat than with a flavorful marinade. Substitute fat-free beef or chicken broth for the red wine if you like.

In a large lock-top plastic bag, combine the shallot, garlic, broth, wine, thyme, mustard, bay leaf, and pepper. Add the steak and mushrooms and seal the bag. Refrigerate for 1–2 hours, turning the bag occasionally.

Remove the steak and mushrooms from the marinade and discard the marinade. Drain and blot dry to remove excess marinade.

Prepare a fire in a charcoal grill or preheat a gas grill or oven broiler. Away from the heat source, lightly coat the grill rack or broiler pan with olive oil cooking spray. Position the grill rack or broiler pan 4–6 inches from the heat source.

Place the steak, mushrooms, and tomatoes on the grill rack or broiler pan and season with the salt. Grill or broil until lightly browned, 4–5 minutes on each side for the steak and about 3 minutes on each side for the mushrooms and the tomatoes. Check the steak for doneness by cutting into the meat or testing with an instant-read thermometer near the thickest part. Rare steaks will be quite red at the center and register 120°–125°F; medium-rare will be red to pink and 130°–135°F, and medium will be just pink and 140°F. Let stand for 5 minutes on a cutting board. Cut the steak on the diagonal across the grain into very thin slices. Slice the mushrooms into thin slices. Divide the meat, mushrooms, and tomatoes among warmed individual plates and serve hot.

1 large shallot, finely chopped

2 cloves garlic, minced

½ cup fat-free, no-salt-added beef or chicken broth

¼ cup dry red wine

1 teaspoon chopped fresh thyme or ½ teaspoon dried thyme

½ teaspoon dry mustard

½ bay leaf

¼ teaspoon freshly ground pepper

¾ lb top round or flank steak, trimmed of visible fat

4 portobello mushrooms, brushed clean and stemmed

Olive oil cooking spray

8 plum (Roma) tomatoes, cored and halved lengthwise

½ teaspoon salt

NUTRIENT ANALYSIS FOR ONE SERVING

Calories 198	**Carbohydrates** 12 g	**Total Fat** 3 g
Protein 23 g	**Fiber** 3 g	**Saturated Fat** 1 g
Sodium 339 mg	**Sugars** 5 g	**Monounsaturated Fat** 1 g
Cholesterol 48 mg		**Polyunsaturated Fat** <1 g

5g

GARLIC MEATBALLS

SERVES 6

- 1 lb 99-percent fat-free ground turkey breast or chicken breast
- ½ cup fresh whole-grain bread crumbs
- ¼ cup grated Parmesan cheese
- ¼ cup plain soy milk
- 1 egg white
- 3 cloves garlic, chopped
- 1 tablespoon olive oil
- 1 teaspoon chopped fresh thyme or ½ teaspoon dried thyme
- 1 teaspoon chopped fresh oregano or ½ teaspoon dried oregano
- ½ teaspoon salt
- ½ teaspoon freshly ground pepper

Savory and fragrant with herbs and garlic, these meatballs are baked, not fried. Serve them with mashed sweet potatoes and steamed broccoli, or with flat whole-wheat noodles and your favorite pasta sauce.

Preheat the oven to 400°F.

In a bowl, combine the turkey, bread crumbs, Parmesan, soy milk, egg white, garlic, olive oil, thyme, oregano, salt, and pepper. Shape the turkey mixture into 24 meatballs about 1 inch in diameter, using about 2 tablespoons per meatball.

Arrange the meatballs on a nonstick baking sheet so they are not touching and bake, turning once halfway through for even browning, until cooked through, 10–12 minutes.

NUTRIENT ANALYSIS FOR ONE SERVING

Calories 148	Carbohydrates 6 g	Total Fat 5 g
Protein 22 g	Fiber 1 g	Saturated Fat 1 g
Sodium 359 mg	Sugars 1 g	Monounsaturated Fat 2 g
Cholesterol 33 mg		Polyunsaturated Fat <1 g

HEARTY PORK STEW

PERCENTAGE OF CALORIES
from total fat 17%
from saturated fat 3%

SERVES 6

In this tangy stew, black beans and lean pork tenderloin are simmered with tomatoes, garlic, and a hint of molasses. Serve with corn bread. You can substitute 1 cup dried beans for the canned beans. (For tips on cooking dried beans, see page 135.)

In a large saucepan, heat the olive oil over medium-high heat. Add the onion and sauté until soft, about 5 minutes. Add the garlic, oregano, cumin, and allspice and cook for 1 minute. Add the tomato and molasses and simmer until the flavors are blended, about 3 minutes. Carefully add the broth and bring to a boil.

Add the pork and black beans and simmer until the pork is just cooked through, about 5 minutes. Season with the salt and pepper, garnish with the cilantro, and serve immediately.

1 tablespoon olive oil

1 yellow onion, chopped

3 cloves garlic, minced

2 teaspoons finely chopped fresh oregano or 1 teaspoon dried oregano

1 teaspoon ground cumin

¼ teaspoon ground allspice

1 large tomato, chopped

1 tablespoon dark molasses

1 cup fat-free, no-salt-added chicken broth

1 lb pork tenderloin, trimmed of visible fat and cut into 1-inch cubes

3 cups canned black beans (about 2 cans, each 15 oz), rinsed and drained

½ teaspoon salt

½ teaspoon freshly ground pepper

1 tablespoon chopped fresh cilantro or parsley

NUTRIENT ANALYSIS FOR ONE SERVING

Calories 245	**Carbohydrates** 26 g	**Total Fat** 5 g
Protein 24 g	**Fiber** 6 g	**Saturated Fat** 1 g
Sodium 409 mg	**Sugars** 8 g	**Monounsaturated Fat** 3 g
Cholesterol 49 mg		**Polyunsaturated Fat** 1 g

SZECHUAN NOODLES WITH SHREDDED BEEF

SERVES 4

For the marinade:

2 tablespoons low-sodium soy sauce

¼ cup fat-free, no-salt-added beef or chicken broth

2 teaspoons peeled and chopped fresh ginger

2 cloves garlic, chopped

1 teaspoon dark honey

2 tablespoons chopped fresh cilantro

¾ lb beef sirloin or eye of round, trimmed of visible fat and cut across the grain into thin strips

4 oz whole-wheat fettuccine

1 teaspoon sesame oil

1 teaspoon olive oil

½ red bell pepper, diced

1 carrot, peeled, halved lengthwise, and thinly sliced on the diagonal

1 celery stalk, halved lengthwise and thinly sliced on the diagonal

½ cup fat-free, no-salt-added beef, chicken, or vegetable broth

1½ teaspoons cornstarch

½ cup bean sprouts

1 small green onion, including tender green parts, thinly sliced on the diagonal

This quick and easy stir-fry made with lean sirloin and a variety of colorful, vitamin-rich vegetables has enough flavorful sauce to coat a mound of steaming noodles. You can substitute pork tenderloin or skinless chicken breast for the beef.

To make the marinade, in a shallow dish, combine the soy sauce, broth, ginger, garlic, honey, and cilantro. Add the beef, turn once to coat, cover, and refrigerate for at least 1 hour and up to 6 hours.

Meanwhile, bring a saucepan three-fourths full of salted water to a boil. Add the fettuccine and cook until al dente, 8–10 minutes. Drain, set aside, and keep warm.

Remove the beef from the marinade and blot dry. Reserve the marinade. In a wok or large nonstick frying pan, heat the oils over medium-high heat. Add the beef and toss and stir for 1 minute. Add the bell pepper, carrot, and celery and cook until the vegetables are tender-crisp. In a small bowl, combine the broth and the cornstarch. Stir well to mix. Add the reserved marinade and the cornstarch mixture to the pan. Stir until the sauce comes to a boil and starts to thicken slightly. Add the bean sprouts and stir to combine and heat through.

Transfer the warm fettuccine to a serving bowl, add the beef-and-vegetable mixture, and garnish with the green onion. Serve immediately.

NUTRIENT ANALYSIS FOR ONE SERVING

Calories 289	**Carbohydrates** 23 g	**Total Fat** 9 g
Protein 30 g	**Fiber** 3 g	**Saturated Fat** 3 g
Sodium 375 mg	**Sugars** 4 g	**Monounsaturated Fat** 4 g
Cholesterol 70 mg		**Polyunsaturated Fat** 1 g

BEANS BOURGUIGNON

SERVES 6

2 tablespoons olive oil

1 yellow onion, chopped

1 carrot, peeled and diced

1 celery stalk, diced

½ cup dry red wine

2½ cups fat-free, no-salt-added chicken or vegetable broth

3 cloves garlic, minced

1 teaspoon chopped fresh thyme

1 bay leaf

½ teaspoon salt

1 cup dried brown lentils, rinsed

1 large tomato, chopped, or 1 cup prepared tomato sauce

8 oz button mushrooms, brushed clean and sliced

3 cups canned low-sodium pinto beans (about 2 cans, each 15 oz), rinsed and drained

2 cups chopped fresh spinach

2 tablespoons chopped fresh parsley

This hearty, meatless version of the classic French dish is packed with the soluble fiber so important for heart health. You can substitute 1 cup dried pinto beans for the canned beans. (For tips on cooking dried beans, see page 135.)

In a large saucepan, heat 1 tablespoon of the olive oil over medium-high heat. Add the onion, carrot, and celery and sauté until the onion is softened, about 5 minutes. Add the wine and cook until the wine is absorbed. Add the broth and ½ cup water and bring to a boil. Add the garlic, thyme, bay leaf, salt, lentils, and tomato. Return to a boil. Reduce the heat to low, cover, and simmer until the lentils are tender, about 25 minutes. Discard the bay leaf.

Meanwhile, in a frying pan over low heat, heat the remaining 1 tablespoon olive oil. Add the mushrooms and sauté until tender, about 5 minutes.

When the lentils are done, add the pinto beans to the saucepan, stir well, and return to a boil. Add the mushrooms and the spinach. Stir to combine and cover for 1 minute to wilt the spinach. Ladle into large shallow soup bowls and garnish with the parsley. Serve immediately.

NUTRIENT ANALYSIS FOR ONE SERVING

Calories 270	Carbohydrates 42 g	Total Fat 3 g
Protein 18 g	Fiber 15 g	Saturated Fat <1 g
Sodium 507 mg	Sugars 5 g	Monounsaturated Fat 3 g
Cholesterol 0 mg		Polyunsaturated Fat <1 g

BLACK BEAN QUESADILLAS

FAT COUNT

9g

PERCENTAGE OF CALORIES
from total fat | 24%
from saturated fat | 5%

SERVES 4

Serve for breakfast, lunch, or dinner; these quesadillas are perfect anytime. For variety, add shredded chicken, use pinto beans in place of the black beans, or substitute whole-wheat flour tortillas.

Preheat the oven to 400°F.

In a sauté pan, heat the olive oil over medium heat. Add the yellow onion and bell pepper and sauté until softened, about 3 minutes. Add the tomatoes and garlic and cook for 2 minutes longer. Add the black beans, chili powder, and salt and cook until the beans are heated through, about 1 minute. Remove from the heat, add the cilantro, and stir to combine.

Spread the bean mixture over 6 of the tortillas, using about ½ cup for each and leaving a ½-inch border at the edges. Sprinkle each with 2 tablespoons of cheese. Brush the edges with water, top each with another tortilla, and gently press the edges of the tortillas together.

Bake until the cheese is melted, about 5 minutes. Cut each quesadilla in half and place 3 halves on each plate. Garnish with the green onion. Serve immediately.

1 tablespoon olive oil

1 yellow onion, chopped

1 green or red bell pepper, seeded and chopped

2 tomatoes, seeded (page 54) and chopped

2 cloves garlic, minced

3 cups canned black beans (about 1½ cans, each 15 oz), drained and partially mashed

2 teaspoons chili powder

½ teaspoon salt

¼ cup chopped fresh cilantro

Twelve 6-inch soft corn tortillas

¾ cup shredded low-fat Cheddar cheese

2 tablespoons chopped green onion

NUTRIENT ANALYSIS FOR ONE SERVING

Calories 339	**Carbohydrates** 41 g	**Total Fat** 9 g
Protein 23 g	**Fiber** 10 g	**Saturated Fat** 2 g
Sodium 506 mg	**Sugars** 6 g	**Monounsaturated Fat** 3 g
Cholesterol 4 mg		**Polyunsaturated Fat** 1 g

POLENTA WITH ROASTED TOMATO SAUCE

FAT COUNT

6g

PERCENTAGE OF CALORIES
| from total fat | 32% |
| from saturated fat | 4% |

SERVES 6

This satisfying vegetarian dish can be served either as a main course or as a generous side dish alongside roast chicken with sautéed spinach or a salad.

Preheat the oven to 450°F.

On a nonstick baking sheet, toss the tomato halves and garlic cloves with 1 tablespoon of the olive oil. Bake until the tomatoes are tender and beginning to brown lightly, about 20 minutes. Set aside to cool slightly.

In a large, heavy saucepan, combine the broth, soy milk, the remaining 1 tablespoon olive oil, and ½ teaspoon of the salt and bring to a boil over medium heat. Whisk in the cornmeal in a slow stream. Reduce the heat to low. Cover and cook, stirring frequently, until the polenta is thick and creamy, about 20 minutes. Remove from the heat and let stand for 10 minutes.

Transfer the roasted tomatoes and garlic to a blender or food processor. Add the chopped basil, pepper, and remaining ½ teaspoon salt. Process until smooth. Transfer the sauce to a small saucepan and heat to a simmer over low heat.

Whisk the ricotta into the polenta and mound on a serving platter. Top with the tomato sauce and garnish with the basil leaves.

3 plum (Roma) tomatoes, cored and halved

2 cloves garlic

2 tablespoons olive oil

3 cups fat-free, no-salt-added chicken or vegetable broth

1 cup low-fat plain soy milk

1 teaspoon salt

1 cup stone-ground cornmeal

2 teaspoons chopped fresh basil or ¾ teaspoon dried basil, plus whole leaves for garnish

¼ teaspoon freshly ground pepper

½ cup fat-free ricotta cheese

NUTRIENT ANALYSIS FOR ONE SERVING

Calories 171	**Carbohydrates** 21 g	**Total Fat** 6 g
Protein 9 g	**Fiber** 4 g	**Saturated Fat** 1 g
Sodium 523 mg	**Sugars** 4 g	**Monounsaturated Fat** 4 g
Cholesterol 0 mg		**Polyunsaturated Fat** <1 g

EGGPLANT PROVENÇALE

SERVES 4

Olive oil cooking spray

2 eggplants, about 1¼ lb each, cut lengthwise in ½-inch slices

1 tablespoon olive oil

½ yellow onion, finely chopped

1 tablespoon balsamic vinegar

1 red bell pepper, seeded and diced

2 large tomatoes, chopped

1 clove garlic, minced

2 teaspoons capers, drained and chopped

3 tablespoons sliced, pitted ripe olives

1 teaspoon chopped fresh thyme or ½ teaspoon dried thyme

¼ teaspoon salt

¼ teaspoon freshly ground pepper

2 tablespoons grated Romano cheese

1 tablespoon chopped fresh basil or parsley

Layers of flavor and loads of antioxidants and fiber make this classic French eggplant dish elegant, delicious, and nutritious. You can make it ahead of time and just pop it in the oven for 20 minutes before serving.

Lightly coat a 1½-qt baking dish with olive oil cooking spray. Prepare a fire in a charcoal grill or preheat a gas grill or oven broiler. Away from the heat source, lightly coat the grill rack or broiler pan with olive oil cooking spray. Position the grill rack or broiler pan 4–6 inches from the heat.

Arrange the eggplant slices on the rack or broiler pan and grill or broil, turning once, until tender and browned, about 3 minutes on each side. Layer half of the slices in the prepared baking dish. Set the rest aside.

Preheat the oven to 350°F.

In a large sauté pan, heat the olive oil over medium heat until hot but not smoking. Add the onion and sauté until golden, about 6 minutes. Add the vinegar and cook until absorbed, about 1 minute. Add the bell pepper and cook until soft, about 3 minutes. Add the tomatoes, garlic, and capers. Cook, stirring occasionally, until the tomatoes are tender, about 5 minutes. Stir in the olives and season with the thyme, salt, and pepper.

Pour half of the sauce over the eggplant and sprinkle with half of the cheese. Add the remaining eggplant slices to the dish and top with the remaining sauce and cheese. Bake until the eggplant is tender when pierced with the tip of a knife and the sauce is bubbling, 15–20 minutes. Garnish with the basil and serve.

NUTRIENT ANALYSIS FOR ONE SERVING

Calories 190	Carbohydrates 33 g	Total Fat 6 g
Protein 6 g	Fiber 9 g	Saturated Fat 1 g
Sodium 331 mg	Sugars 19 g	Monounsaturated Fat 3 g
Cholesterol 3 mg		Polyunsaturated Fat 1 g

PASTA WITH GRILLED TOMATOES & FETA

FAT COUNT

10g

PERCENTAGE OF CALORIES
from total fat   24%
from saturated fat   7%

SERVES 4

This hearty pasta dish has plenty of chunky tomato sauce. Great on a cold night, it's also perfect midday fare. Served with a piece of fish or chicken, it makes a side dish for eight. Fettuccine, linguine, and rigatoni all work well here.

Prepare a fire in a charcoal grill or preheat a gas grill or oven broiler. Position the grill rack or broiler pan 4–6 inches from the heat source.

Insert a toothpick into the side of each onion slice to hold the rings together. Lightly brush the 1 tablespoon olive oil on both sides of the onion slices and tomato halves. Place the onion slices and tomatoes on the grill rack or broiler pan. Grill or broil until browned, about 4 minutes on each side. Transfer to a cutting board and let cool.

Bring a saucepan three-fourths full of lightly salted water to a boil. Add the fettuccine and cook until al dente, 8–10 minutes. Drain and set aside.

Meanwhile, remove the toothpicks from the onion slices and chop the slices into ½-inch pieces. Chop the tomatoes coarsely. In a large sauté pan, heat the remaining 1 teaspoon olive oil over medium-high heat. Add the tomatoes, onions, garlic, oregano, and pepper. Cook until the sauce is bubbling, about 3 minutes. Remove from the heat. Add the fettuccine and toss gently until the pasta is well coated with sauce. Transfer to a serving bowl and sprinkle with the feta and parsley. Serve hot.

2 red onions, peeled and sliced horizontally in ½-inch slices

1 tablespoon olive oil, plus 1 teaspoon

8 firm but ripe tomatoes, about 2 lb total weight, cored and halved horizontally

8 oz whole-wheat pasta

2 cloves garlic, minced

1 tablespoon chopped fresh oregano

½ teaspoon freshly ground pepper

4 oz crumbled reduced-fat feta cheese

1 tablespoon chopped fresh parsley

NUTRIENT ANALYSIS FOR ONE SERVING

Calories 379	**Carbohydrates** 64 g	**Total Fat** 10 g
Protein 18 g	**Fiber** 8 g	**Saturated Fat** 3 g
Sodium 409 mg	**Sugars** 15 g	**Monounsaturated Fat** 3 g
Cholesterol 10 mg		**Polyunsaturated Fat** 1 g

FAT COUNT

7g

PERCENTAGE OF CALORIES
from total fat   25%
from saturated fat   4%

GARDEN ORZO SALAD

SERVES 6

2 tablespoons olive oil

½ yellow onion, minced

1 clove garlic, minced

1 cup vegetable or chicken broth

6 oz orzo

1½ cups canned cannellini or
    Great Northern beans (about one
    15-oz can), rinsed and drained

2 cups cherry tomatoes, halved

1 large cucumber, peeled, seeded,
    and diced

½ cup sliced pitted Kalamata olives

1 teaspoon grated lemon zest

1 tablespoon lemon juice

2 tablespoons chopped fresh dill

½ teaspoon salt

¼ teaspoon freshly ground pepper

Cannellini beans and tiny grains of pasta soak up a rich broth, then meld with high-fiber fresh ingredients. Serve with tomato soup or gazpacho. You can substitute ½ cup dried beans for the canned beans. (For tips on cooking dried beans, see page 135.)

In a large saucepan, heat the olive oil over medium-high heat. Add the onion and sauté until soft, about 3 minutes. Add the garlic and sauté for 1 minute longer. Add the broth and bring to a boil. Add the orzo, cover, and simmer until the pasta is just tender, about 7 minutes. Remove from the heat and let stand until almost all of the liquid is absorbed, about 3 minutes. Transfer to a large bowl, add the cannellini beans and tomatoes, and stir to combine. Let cool slightly.

Stir in the cucumber, olives, lemon zest and juice, dill, salt, and pepper. Serve immediately.

NUTRIENT ANALYSIS FOR ONE SERVING

Calories 237	Carbohydrates 37 g	Total Fat 7 g
Protein 9 g	Fiber 6 g	Saturated Fat 1 g
Sodium 456 mg	Sugars 3 g	Monounsaturated Fat 1 g
Cholesterol 0 mg		Polyunsaturated Fat 4 g

HOPPIN' JOHN

SERVES 4

PERCENTAGE OF CALORIES
from total fat ▭ 20%
from saturated fat ▏ 3%

Traditionally enriched with smoked meat, this meatless version of a Southern classic is full of protein and heart-healthy fiber from legumes and wilted greens. Serve this brothy dish in shallow bowls with wedges of corn bread.

In a large pot or Dutch oven, heat the olive oil over medium heat. Add the onions and cook, stirring occasionally, until soft, about 5 minutes, then add the garlic and cook until onions are golden, about 5 minutes longer. Add the broth and ½ cup water and bring to a boil. Add the black-eyed peas, bay leaf, and ¼ teaspoon of the salt. Bring to a boil. Cover, reduce the heat, and simmer for 30 minutes. Add the rice and return the mixture to a boil, then reduce the heat, cover, and simmer until the rice and peas are tender, about 30 minutes. (Add more water if needed.) Discard the bay leaf.

Remove from the heat and stir in the mustard greens, the remaining ¼ teaspoon salt, the thyme, and the pepper. Cover and let stand for 2 minutes, then serve immediately.

1 tablespoon olive oil

2 yellow onions, chopped

3 cloves garlic, minced

4 cups fat-free, no-salt-added chicken or vegetable broth

¾ cup dried black-eyed peas

1 bay leaf

½ teaspoon salt

¾ cup brown rice, preferably basmati

3 cups coarsely chopped mustard greens or spinach

1 teaspoon chopped fresh thyme or ½ teaspoon dried thyme

½ teaspoon freshly ground pepper

NUTRIENT ANALYSIS FOR ONE SERVING

Calories 358	**Carbohydrates** 54 g	**Total Fat** 8 g
Protein 17 g	**Fiber** 8 g	**Saturated Fat** 1 g
Sodium 492 mg	**Sugars** 7 g	**Monounsaturated Fat** 5 g
Cholesterol 0 mg		**Polyunsaturated Fat** <1 g

MUSHROOM VEGGIE BURGER

SERVES 4

1 cup fat-free, no-salt-added chicken or vegetable broth

¼ cup brown rice, preferably basmati

3 tablespoons fine-grind bulgur

3 oz button mushrooms, brushed clean and finely chopped

¼ cup finely chopped onion

¼ cup dried bread crumbs, or more as needed

2 tablespoons grated Parmesan or Romano cheese

1 egg white

1 tablespoon chopped fresh parsley

1 teaspoon chopped fresh basil or ½ teaspoon dried basil

½ teaspoon chopped fresh thyme or ¼ teaspoon dried thyme

¼ teaspoon salt

1 tablespoon olive oil

4 small whole-grain buns, split and toasted

4 tomato slices

4 lettuce leaves

These meatless burgers are loaded with flavor and can be baked, grilled, or sautéed. They're also excellent made with portobellos or shiitakes in place of the button mushrooms.

In a saucepan, bring the broth to a boil. Add the rice and bulgur. Cover, reduce the heat, and simmer gently until the rice is almost tender, about 20 minutes. Remove from the heat and let steam, covered, for 10 minutes.

In a bowl, combine the mushrooms, onion, bread crumbs, cheese, egg white, parsley, basil, thyme, and salt. Add the cooked grains and stir well. If the mixture is too wet, add 1 tablespoon bread crumbs. If the mixture is too dry, add 1–2 teaspoons water.

Using only ½ cup per burger, shape the mushroom mixture into patties about 3 inches in diameter.

In a nonstick sauté pan, heat the olive oil over medium heat. Add the burgers and cook until golden brown, 2–3 minutes on each side. Alternatively, bake the burgers: Preheat the oven to 375°F. Place the burgers on a lightly oiled baking sheet. Using the 1 tablespoon olive oil, brush the tops lightly and bake for 10 minutes. Turn the burgers, brush with more olive oil, and bake for 5 minutes longer.

Transfer the burgers to the toasted buns and garnish with the tomato slices and lettuce leaves.

NUTRIENT ANALYSIS FOR ONE SERVING

Calories 280	**Carbohydrates** 47 g	**Total Fat** 7 g
Protein 10 g	**Fiber** 6 g	**Saturated Fat** 1 g
Sodium 593 mg	**Sugars** 5 g	**Monounsaturated Fat** 4 g
Cholesterol 2 mg		**Polyunsaturated Fat** 2 g

PENNE WITH CANNELLINI & WILTED ESCAROLE

FAT COUNT

6g

PERCENTAGE OF CALORIES
from total fat　　　　　　 14%
from saturated fat　　　　 5%

SERVES 4

Cannellini are white beans used in many classic Italian dishes. If you can't find them, Great Northern white beans work well. You can substitute ½ cup dried cannellini beans for the canned beans. (For tips on cooking dried beans, see page 135.)

Bring a saucepan three-fourths full of water to a boil. Add the pasta and cook until al dente, 10–12 minutes. Drain and set aside.

Heat the olive oil in a large saucepan over medium heat. Add the tomatoes and garlic and cook until the tomatoes are tender, about 3 minutes. Add the cannellini beans and the broth and bring to a boil. Add the escarole, salt, and pepper and cook until the greens just begin to wilt, about 2 minutes.

Add the pasta, toss well, and cook until the pasta is heated through.

Divide the pasta evenly among warmed shallow individual bowls. Top with the grated Parmesan and serve.

8 oz whole-wheat penne or rigatoni

1 tablespoon olive oil

2 plum (Roma) tomatoes, seeded (page 54) and coarsely chopped

3 cloves garlic, chopped

1½ cups canned cannellini beans (about one 15-oz can), rinsed and drained

1 cup fat-free, no-salt-added chicken or vegetable broth

2 cups chopped fresh escarole or Swiss chard

½ teaspoon salt

¼ teaspoon freshly ground pepper

2 tablespoons grated Parmesan cheese

NUTRIENT ANALYSIS FOR ONE SERVING

Calories 355	**Carbohydrates** 62 g	**Total Fat** 6 g
Protein 17 g	**Fiber** 6 g	**Saturated Fat** 1 g
Sodium 426 mg	**Sugars** 3 g	**Monounsaturated Fat** 3 g
Cholesterol 4 mg		**Polyunsaturated Fat** 1 g

SIDE DISHES

Roasted Asparagus with Lemon & Parmesan, 108

3g

PERCENTAGE OF CALORIES
from total fat 34%
from saturated fat 6%

BABY CARROTS WITH LEMON & WALNUTS

SERVES 6

2 tablespoons chopped walnuts, toasted (page 138)

1 teaspoon chopped fresh parsley

2 teaspoons grated lemon zest

1 tablespoon finely chopped raisins

½ cup fat-free, no-salt-added chicken or vegetable broth

1 tablespoon fresh lemon juice

1 teaspoon chopped fresh dill or ½ teaspoon dried dill

4 cups diagonally sliced baby carrots

½ teaspoon salt

The simple additions of fresh herbs, grated lemon zest, and toasted nuts turn an everyday vegetable into something elegant. Use dried figs in place of the raisins, if you like, for a new flavor dimension.

In a bowl, combine the walnuts, parsley, lemon zest, and raisins. Set aside.

In a saucepan, combine the broth, lemon juice, and dill and heat over medium-high heat. When the liquid is just beginning to boil, add the carrots. Cover and steam until the carrots are tender-crisp, about 3 minutes. Uncover the pan and continue to cook, shaking the pan frequently, until the carrots are tender and the broth is nearly evaporated, about 3 minutes longer. Transfer to a bowl, add the salt and the walnut mixture, and toss to combine. Serve immediately.

NUTRIENT ANALYSIS FOR ONE SERVING

Calories 78	Carbohydrates 12 g	Total Fat 3 g
Protein 3 g	Fiber 2 g	Saturated Fat <1 g
Sodium 209 mg	Sugars 6 g	Monounsaturated Fat <1 g
Cholesterol 0 mg		Polyunsaturated Fat 2 g

BARLEY RISOTTO WITH ONION & MUSHROOMS

FAT COUNT

3g

PERCENTAGE OF CALORIES
from total fat 18%
from saturated fat 3%

SERVES 8

Pearl barley has been polished and steamed so that it cooks quickly. Here, it's prepared risotto style, by lightly toasting it in olive oil with vegetables before adding the broth. But instead of stirring constantly at the stove, you finish it in the oven.

Preheat the oven to 350°F. Lightly coat a 2-qt baking dish with olive oil cooking spray.

In a saucepan, heat 2 teaspoons of the oil over medium heat. Add the onion and sauté until softened and beginning to brown, about 7 minutes. Add the carrot and celery and cook for 1 minute. Add the barley and oregano and sauté for 1 minute, stirring to coat the barley. Add the broth and 1½ cups water and bring to a boil. Remove from the heat and carefully transfer the mixture to the prepared baking dish. Cover and bake until the barley is tender and the liquid is almost absorbed, about 50 minutes.

Just before the risotto is done, heat the remaining 2 teaspoons oil in a nonstick frying pan over medium-high heat. Add the mushrooms, season with the salt and pepper, and sauté until tender, about 5 minutes. Remove from the heat. Add the mushrooms, Parmesan, and parsley to the risotto and stir gently to combine. Serve hot.

Olive oil cooking spray

4 teaspoons olive oil or canola oil

1 yellow onion, chopped

1 carrot, peeled, halved lengthwise, and thinly sliced

1 celery stalk, diced

1 cup pearl barley, rinsed

1 teaspoon chopped fresh oregano or ½ teaspoon dried oregano

2 cups fat-free, no-salt-added chicken or vegetable broth

½ lb cremini mushrooms, brushed clean and sliced

½ teaspoon salt

½ teaspoon freshly ground pepper

¼ cup grated Parmesan cheese

2 tablespoons chopped fresh parsley

NUTRIENT ANALYSIS FOR ONE SERVING

Calories 146	**Carbohydrates** 24 g	**Total Fat** 3 g
Protein 6 g	**Fiber** 5 g	**Saturated Fat** <1 g
Sodium 174 mg	**Sugars** 3 g	**Monounsaturated Fat** 2 g
Cholesterol 2 mg		**Polyunsaturated Fat** <1 g

3g

PERCENTAGE OF CALORIES
from total fat — 34%
from saturated fat — 6%

BRAISED KALE WITH CELERY ROOT

SERVES 6

1 tablespoon olive oil

1 small celery root, peeled and cut into matchsticks (about 1¼ cups)

1 shallot, minced

2 cloves garlic, minced

1 lb kale, thick ribs and stems cut away, leaves sliced into ½-inch strips (about 6 cups)

¼ cup fat-free, no-salt-added chicken or vegetable broth

½ teaspoon salt

¼ teaspoon freshly ground pepper

Swiss chard or spinach can replace the kale in this flavorful side dish. To cut the greens into strips, stack the leaves and roll tightly lengthwise into a cylinder, then slice crosswise into ½-inch pieces. If you can't find celery root, celery works well.

In large nonstick frying pan, heat the olive oil over high heat. Add the celery root and shallot and sauté until the celery root is nearly tender, about 4 minutes. Add the garlic and cook for 30 seconds. Add the kale and the broth and bring to a boil. Cover and cook until the kale is wilted and tender, about 3 minutes.

Season with the salt and pepper. Serve warm.

NUTRIENT ANALYSIS FOR ONE SERVING

Calories 79	**Carbohydrates** 12 g	**Total Fat** 3 g
Protein 3 g	**Fiber** 2 g	**Saturated Fat** <1 g
Sodium 176 mg	**Sugars** 3 g	**Monounsaturated Fat** 2 g
Cholesterol 0 mg		**Polyunsaturated Fat** <1 g

CORN PUDDING

SERVES 6

PERCENTAGE OF CALORIES
from total fat 30%
from saturated fat 8%

A classic comfort dish, this creamy pudding is a perfect accompaniment to grilled or roast chicken. Fresh sweet corn delivers the fullest flavor, but you can use thawed frozen kernels in the winter months.

Preheat the oven to 350°F. Lightly coat a 2-qt baking dish with olive oil cooking spray.

In a nonstick saucepan, heat the oil over medium-high heat. Add the onion and bell pepper and sauté for about 3 minutes. Add 1 cup of the corn, the basil, salt, pepper, and nutmeg and cook for 1 minute. Remove from the heat. Add the cornmeal, stir to combine, and transfer to a bowl. Let cool.

In a blender, combine the milk, egg whites, honey, and the remaining ½ cup corn. Process until puréed. Add to the cooled vegetable mixture, stir just to combine, and pour the mixture into the prepared baking dish.

Bake until the pudding is puffed and just set, 35–40 minutes. Let cool slightly and serve hot.

Olive oil cooking spray

1 tablespoon olive oil or canola oil

½ yellow onion, chopped

½ red bell pepper, diced

1½ cups fresh corn kernels, cut from 3 ears of corn

1 tablespoon chopped fresh basil or 1 teaspoon dried basil

½ teaspoon salt

¼ teaspoon freshly ground pepper

⅛ teaspoon ground nutmeg

3 tablespoons stone-ground cornmeal

2 cups 1-percent low-fat milk

2 large egg whites

1 teaspoon dark honey

NUTRIENT ANALYSIS FOR ONE SERVING

Calories 119	**Carbohydrates** 17 g	**Total Fat** 4 g
Protein 6 g	**Fiber** 2 g	**Saturated Fat** 1 g
Sodium 166 mg	**Sugars** 7 g	**Monounsaturated Fat** 2 g
Cholesterol 5 mg		**Polyunsaturated Fat** <1 g

ROASTED ASPARAGUS WITH LEMON & PARMESAN

SERVES 4

1 lb asparagus spears, tough ends snapped off

1 teaspoon extra-virgin olive oil

¼ teaspoon salt

1 teaspoon fresh lemon juice

1 teaspoon grated Parmesan cheese

⅛ teaspoon freshly ground pepper

Just a few basic ingredients and a short roasting time are all you need for the tastiest asparagus ever. The key to perfectly roasted vegetables is a very hot oven. The small amount of grated Parmesan adds flavor but only a tiny bit of fat.

Place a rack in the lower third of the oven and preheat to 500°F.

Toss the asparagus with the olive oil on a baking sheet. Sprinkle with the salt. Roast the asparagus, shaking the pan halfway through the cooking time to turn it, until tender and lightly browned, about 5 minutes for thin spears and about 8 minutes for thicker spears.

Remove from the oven and transfer to a serving platter. Sprinkle with the lemon juice, Parmesan, and pepper and toss to combine. Serve hot or at room temperature.

NUTRIENT ANALYSIS FOR ONE SERVING

Calories 43	**Carbohydrates** 5 g	**Total Fat** 1 g
Protein 3 g	**Fiber** 2 g	**Saturated Fat** <1 g
Sodium 155 mg	**Sugars** 3 g	**Monounsaturated Fat** 1 g
Cholesterol <1 mg		**Polyunsaturated Fat** <1 g

ROASTED EGGPLANT WITH MINT & TOMATOES

SERVES 4

A little chopped fresh mint, some juicy ripe tomatoes, and a spoonful of rich balsamic vinegar lift roasted eggplant to new heights in this easy side dish. If you can't find cherry tomatoes, use 1 cup diced plum (Roma) tomatoes.

Place a rack in the lower third of the oven and preheat to 450°F. Lightly coat a baking sheet with olive oil cooking spray.

Spread the eggplant cubes in a single layer on the prepared baking sheet. Drizzle with the olive oil and toss gently. Roast for 10 minutes. Turn the eggplant and continue roasting until softened and lightly golden, about 10 minutes longer. Set aside and let cool.

In a bowl, combine the cooled eggplant, tomatoes, green onion, and mint. Drizzle with the vinegar, season with the salt and pepper, and toss gently. Serve warm or at room temperature.

Olive oil cooking spray

1 large eggplant, about 1½ lb, cut into ½-inch cubes

2 teaspoons olive oil

1 cup cherry tomatoes, halved

2 tablespoons chopped green onion, including tender green parts

2 tablespoons chopped fresh mint

1 tablespoon balsamic vinegar

½ teaspoon salt

¼ teaspoon freshly ground pepper

NUTRIENT ANALYSIS FOR ONE SERVING

Calories 77	**Carbohydrates** 13 g	**Total Fat** 3 g
Protein 2 g	**Fiber** 5 g	**Saturated Fat** <1 g
Sodium 306 mg	**Sugars** 8 g	**Monounsaturated Fat** 2 g
Cholesterol 0 mg		**Polyunsaturated Fat** <1 g

2g

PARMESAN TOMATOES

SERVES 4

Olive oil cooking spray

8 firm but ripe plum (Roma) or beefsteak tomatoes, about 1½ lb total weight

¼ cup dried bread crumbs, preferably Italian seasoned, or more as needed

2 tablespoons grated Parmesan cheese

1 large clove garlic, chopped

1 tablespoon chopped fresh parsley

1 teaspoon chopped fresh basil, thyme, or oregano or ½ teaspoon dried

1 teaspoon olive oil

¼ teaspoon freshly ground pepper

⅛ teaspoon salt

These tomatoes topped with herbs and Parmesan are the perfect accompaniment to a summer meal of grilled vegetables and chicken. Tomatoes are rich in the antioxidant lycopene, which is most readily absorbed by the body when cooked.

Preheat the oven to 425°F. Lightly coat an 8-inch square baking dish with olive oil cooking spray.

Remove a thin slice from the bottom of each tomato so it will stand upright. Slice the tops from the tomatoes and discard. Scoop out about 1 teaspoon of pulp from each tomato and place the pulp in a bowl. Arrange the tomatoes upright in the prepared baking dish.

Add the bread crumbs, Parmesan, garlic, parsley, basil, olive oil, pepper, and salt to the bowl with the tomato pulp and stir to combine. The mixture should look like wet sand. If it is too wet, add a few bread crumbs. If it is too dry, add a few drops of water. Gently mound a heaping tablespoon of topping into the cavity of each tomato.

Bake until the tomatoes are tender and the topping is lightly golden, about 10 minutes. Serve hot.

NUTRIENT ANALYSIS FOR ONE SERVING

Calories 59	**Carbohydrates** 8 g	**Total Fat** 2 g
Protein 3 g	**Fiber** 2 g	**Saturated Fat** <1 g
Sodium 134 mg	**Sugars** 4 g	**Monounsaturated Fat** 1 g
Cholesterol 2 mg		**Polyunsaturated Fat** <1 g

2g

COUNTRY-STYLE LENTILS

SERVES 6

1 tablespoon extra-virgin olive oil

½ yellow onion, finely chopped

½ teaspoon celery seeds

1 teaspoon chopped fresh thyme
or ½ teaspoon dried thyme

1 bay leaf

2 cups fat-free, no-salt-added
chicken or vegetable broth

1 cup dried brown lentils, rinsed

2 green onions, including tender
green parts, chopped

1 tablespoon chopped fresh
parsley

1 tablespoon balsamic vinegar or
2 teaspoons red wine vinegar

½ teaspoon salt

Earthy brown lentils simmered in a sumptuous broth make a satisfying side dish with rich color and deep flavor. Serve alongside roast chicken or with Mustard-Braised Cod with Wilted Chard (page 68).

In a saucepan, heat the olive oil over medium-high heat. Add the yellow onion and sauté until soft, about 4 minutes. Add the celery seeds, thyme, and bay leaf and cook for 1 minute longer. Carefully add the broth and ¼ cup water and bring to a boil.

Add the lentils and reduce the heat to medium-low. Cover and simmer until the lentils are tender, about 20 minutes. Discard the bay leaf. Add the green onions, parsley, vinegar, and salt. Stir to combine and cook for about 1 minute longer to allow the flavors to blend. Serve hot.

NUTRIENT ANALYSIS FOR ONE SERVING

Calories 81	**Carbohydrates** 14 g	**Total Fat** 2 g
Protein 7 g	**Fiber** 6 g	**Saturated Fat** <1 g
Sodium 199 mg	**Sugars** <1 g	**Monounsaturated Fat** 2 g
Cholesterol 0 mg		**Polyunsaturated Fat** <1 g

CUBAN-STYLE BLACK BEANS

SERVES 8

FAT COUNT

2 g

PERCENTAGE OF CALORIES
from total fat 15%
from saturated fat 4%

Serve these full-flavored beans with grilled chicken, or wrap them in a whole-wheat tortilla to make a vegetarian burrito. You can substitute 1 cup dried black beans for the canned beans. (For tips on how to cook dried beans, see page 135.)

In a saucepan, heat the olive oil over medium heat. Add the onion and bell pepper and sauté until the vegetables are soft, about 5 minutes.

Add the tomato, garlic, bay leaf, cumin, oregano, salt, pepper, and coriander and cook until the tomato softens, about 3 minutes.

Carefully add the broth and bring to a simmer. Add the black beans, return to a simmer, and cook over low heat until the beans are heated through, about 6 minutes. Discard the bay leaf. Stir in the vinegar and chopped cilantro. Serve hot.

1 tablespoon olive oil

1 yellow onion, chopped

1 green bell pepper, seeded and diced

1 large tomato, chopped

3 cloves garlic, chopped

1 bay leaf

1 teaspoon ground cumin

1 teaspoon chopped fresh oregano or ½ teaspoon dried oregano

¼ teaspoon salt

½ teaspoon freshly ground pepper

½ teaspoon ground coriander

¾ cup fat-free, no-salt-added chicken or vegetable broth

3 cups canned black beans (about 2 cans, each 15 oz), rinsed and drained

1 tablespoon red wine vinegar or balsamic vinegar

1 tablespoon chopped fresh cilantro

NUTRIENT ANALYSIS FOR ONE SERVING

Calories 99	**Carbohydrates** 16 g	**Total Fat** 2 g
Protein 5 g	**Fiber** 4 g	**Saturated Fat** <1 g
Sodium 195 mg	**Sugars** 3 g	**Monounsaturated Fat** 1 g
Cholesterol 0 mg		**Polyunsaturated Fat** <1 g

BULGUR SALAD WITH CUMIN & GARLIC

FAT COUNT

1g

PERCENTAGE OF CALORIES
from total fat ▢ 6%
from saturated fat ▮ 3%

SERVES 4

Bulgur is wheat that has been cracked, parboiled, and ground into fine, medium, or coarse grains. It's most widely used in tabbouleh, a popular Middle Eastern salad, although there are many variations, including this salad with yogurt and spices.

In a saucepan, bring the broth to a boil over high heat. Stir in the cumin, garlic, and red pepper flakes, if using. Remove from the heat. Add the bulgur and stir well to combine. Cover and let stand until the bulgur is plumped and tender, about 30 minutes.

Transfer the bulgur to a bowl. Let cool for 5 minutes. Add the lemon juice, yogurt, dill, parsley, and cucumber. Serve warm or chilled.

1½ cups fat-free, no-salt-added chicken or vegetable broth

¼ teaspoon ground cumin

1 clove garlic, minced

⅛ teaspoon red pepper flakes (optional)

1 cup medium-grind bulgur

1 tablespoon fresh lemon juice

¼ cup low-fat or nonfat plain yogurt

1 tablespoon chopped fresh dill or 1 teaspoon dried dill

1 tablespoon chopped fresh parsley

¼ cup diced cucumber

NUTRIENT ANALYSIS FOR ONE SERVING

Calories 140	**Carbohydrates** 30 g	**Total Fat** 1 g
Protein 5 g	**Fiber** 7 g	**Saturated Fat** <1 g
Sodium 185 mg	**Sugars** 2 g	**Monounsaturated Fat** <1 g
Cholesterol <1 mg		**Polyunsaturated Fat** <1 g

SPICY GREENS WITH SUN-DRIED TOMATOES

SERVES 4

1 tablespoon olive oil

½ red onion, chopped

½ cup chopped sun-dried tomatoes, plumped in warm water

2 tablespoons balsamic vinegar or red wine vinegar

1 clove garlic, chopped

1 lb fresh kale or other greens such as collard or mustard, thick ribs and stems cut away, and leaves chopped

½ teaspoon salt

¼ teaspoon freshly ground pepper

Be sure to swirl fresh greens in plenty of cold water to ensure a good cleaning—quick rinsing doesn't do the trick. If you don't have sun-dried tomatoes on hand, use the same amount of chopped, seeded (page 54) tomatoes.

In a large saucepan or Dutch oven, heat the olive oil over medium heat. Add the onion and sauté until soft, about 4 minutes.

Add the sun-dried tomatoes, vinegar, and garlic and mix well. Add the greens, one-third at a time, pressing them down as they begin to wilt. Season with the salt and pepper. Reduce the heat to medium-low and cook, uncovered, until the greens are tender, about 8 minutes. Serve hot.

NUTRIENT ANALYSIS FOR ONE SERVING

Calories 102	Carbohydrates 16 g	Total Fat 4 g
Protein 4 g	Fiber 3 g	Saturated Fat <1 g
Sodium 197 mg	Sugars 6 g	Monounsaturated Fat 3 g
Cholesterol 0 mg		Polyunsaturated Fat <1 g

ARTICHOKES WITH SWEET ONION VINAIGRETTE

FAT COUNT **3**g

PERCENTAGE OF CALORIES
from total fat　34%
from saturated fat　11%

SERVES 8

This is a great make-ahead dish because it can be served either warm or cold. You may want to make a double batch of the dressing—sweet roasted onion adds depth to a vinaigrette you can use on many other vegetable dishes and salads.

Preheat the oven to 400°F. Working with 1 artichoke at a time, snap off any tough outer leaves and trim the stem flush with the base. Cut off the top one-third of the leaves with a serrated knife, and trim off any remaining thorns with kitchen scissors. Cut the artichoke in half lengthwise. Using a melon baller or metal spoon, scoop out the fuzzy choke, then squeeze some lemon juice into the cavity. Repeat with the remaining artichokes.

Pour the wine, if using, into a saucepan large enough to hold the artichokes. Add the artichokes and fill the pan with water about halfway. Cover and bring to a boil. Reduce the heat to a simmer and steam until the artichokes are tender, 25–30 minutes. Remove and let cool.

Meanwhile, lightly coat a baking sheet with cooking spray. Cut the onion into 8 wedges and place them on the prepared baking sheet. Drizzle with the 1 teaspoon olive oil. Roast for 15 minutes. Turn the wedges and roast until browned, about 15 minutes longer. Set aside to cool.

In a food processor, combine the roasted onion, yogurt, ¼ cup water, Parmesan, mustard, vinegar, thyme, salt, and pepper. Process until smooth and thick, about 3 minutes. With the machine running, add the remaining 1 tablespoon olive oil in a steady, thin stream. Serve 2 tablespoons of the dressing with each artichoke half.

- 4 large artichokes
- 1 lemon, halved
- ¼ cup dry white wine (optional)
- Olive oil cooking spray
- 1 large yellow onion
- 1 teaspoon olive oil, plus 1 tablespoon
- ¼ cup nonfat plain yogurt
- 2 tablespoons grated Parmesan cheese
- 1 tablespoon Dijon mustard
- 2 tablespoons balsamic or red wine vinegar
- 1 teaspoon chopped fresh thyme or ½ teaspoon dried thyme
- ¼ teaspoon salt
- ¼ teaspoon freshly ground pepper

NUTRIENT ANALYSIS FOR ONE SERVING

Calories 79	**Carbohydrates** 12 g	**Total Fat** 3 g
Protein 4 g	**Fiber** 5 g	**Saturated Fat** 1 g
Sodium 226 mg	**Sugars** 2 g	**Monounsaturated Fat** 2 g
Cholesterol 1 mg		**Polyunsaturated Fat** <1 g

DESSERTS & SNACKS

Chocolate Hazelnut Biscotti, 129

BAKED APPLES WITH MAPLE NUT CRUMBLE

SERVES 8

Cooking spray

4 tart apples, peeled, halved, cored, and cut into ¼-inch slices

1 tablespoon fresh lemon juice

¼ cup pure maple syrup

2 tablespoons chopped dried cranberries

1 teaspoon vanilla extract

½ teaspoon ground cinnamon

Pinch of salt

For the topping:

½ cup old-fashioned rolled oats

¼ cup unbleached all-purpose flour

¼ cup chopped walnuts

¾ teaspoon ground cinnamon

½ teaspoon ground cardamom

¼ teaspoon salt

1 tablespoon plus 1½ teaspoons canola oil or olive oil

½ teaspoon vanilla extract

2 large egg whites

¼ cup pure maple syrup

Granny Smith or Fuji apples work especially well in this old-fashioned dessert that's a delight warm from the oven, with the flavor of maple enhancing both the juicy apples and the nutty puffed topping. Honey can replace the maple syrup.

Preheat the oven to 350°F. Lightly coat a 9-inch square baking pan or a 2-qt baking dish with cooking spray.

In a bowl, toss the apple slices with the lemon juice. Add the maple syrup, cranberries, vanilla, cinnamon, and salt and toss well to combine. Spoon the apple mixture into the prepared baking pan or dish. Set aside.

To make the topping, in a bowl, stir together the oats, flour, walnuts, cinnamon, cardamom, and salt. Add the oil and vanilla and toss well to distribute evenly.

In a spotlessly clean bowl or in the bowl of a stand mixer, beat the egg whites at high speed until soft peaks form. Slowly add the maple syrup, continuing to beat until the egg whites return to soft peaks. Carefully fold the egg whites into the dry ingredients. Quickly spread the topping over the apple mixture. Bake until the topping is puffed and lightly golden, about 30 minutes. Serve warm.

NUTRIENT ANALYSIS FOR ONE SERVING

Calories 185	Carbohydrates 33 g	Total Fat 5 g
Protein 3 g	Fiber 3 g	Saturated Fat <1 g
Sodium 163 mg	Sugars 22 g	Monounsaturated Fat 2 g
Cholesterol 0 mg		Polyunsaturated Fat 2 g

BANANA BRAN MUFFINS

PERCENTAGE OF CALORIES
from total fat　　32%
from saturated fat　　4%

MAKES 16 MINIATURE MUFFINS

Don't let their miniature size fool you. These chewy golden muffins, studded with fruit and nuts, are big on flavor and high in fiber. Experiment by substituting different dried fruits, berries, or nuts.

Preheat the oven to 375°F. Lightly coat 16 miniature muffin cups with cooking spray.

In a bowl, whisk together the oil, honey, egg whites, bananas, and vanilla. Set aside.

In another bowl, combine the bran, flours, cornmeal, flaxseed, baking soda, and salt. Stir to mix well. Add the banana mixture and stir just to combine. Add the cranberries, walnuts, and orange zest and stir just to combine.

Place about 2 tablespoons batter in each muffin cup. Bake until the muffins are puffed, golden, and firm to the touch. Transfer to a wire rack to cool.

Cooking spray

3 tablespoons canola oil or olive oil

¼ cup dark honey

2 large egg whites

2 ripe bananas, mashed

½ teaspoon vanilla extract

1 cup wheat bran

½ cup unbleached all-purpose flour

¼ cup whole-wheat flour

2 tablespoons stone-ground cornmeal

2 tablespoons freshly ground flaxseed

¾ teaspoon baking soda

¼ teaspoon salt

½ cup dried cranberries, chopped

3 tablespoons chopped walnuts, toasted (page 138)

1 teaspoon grated orange or lemon zest

NUTRIENT ANALYSIS PER MUFFIN

Calories 112	**Carbohydrates** 19 g	**Total Fat** 4 g
Protein 2 g	**Fiber** 3 g	**Saturated Fat** <1 g
Sodium 141 mg	**Sugars** 9 g	**Monounsaturated Fat** 2 g
Cholesterol 0 mg		**Polyunsaturated Fat** 1 g

BLUEBERRY GINGERBREAD

SERVES 12

Cooking spray

1 cup all-purpose flour

1 cup whole-wheat flour

2 teaspoons baking powder

½ teaspoon baking soda

¼ teaspoon salt

2 teaspoons ground ginger

1 teaspoon ground cinnamon

⅛ teaspoon ground cloves

⅔ cup low-fat plain soy milk

½ cup dark honey

⅓ cup molasses

¼ cup canola oil or olive oil

1 large egg

½ teaspoon vanilla extract

½ cup dried or fresh blueberries

The spin on this moist, dark, spicy cake is the addition of antioxidant-rich blueberries for bursts of sweet fruit flavor. Use dried cranberries instead if you like tart with your sweet. This is a cake worthy of any holiday table.

Preheat the oven to 350°F. Lightly coat an 8-inch square baking pan with cooking spray.

In a bowl, stir together the flours, baking powder, baking soda, salt, ginger, cinnamon, and cloves. Set aside.

In another bowl, whisk together the soy milk, honey, molasses, and oil. Beat in the egg and vanilla. Make a well in the dry ingredients and pour in the liquid mixture. Add the blueberries to the well and stir just to combine.

Pour the batter into the prepared pan. Bake until a toothpick inserted into the center of the cake comes out clean, about 25 minutes. Transfer to a wire rack to cool. Cut into 12 pieces and serve warm.

NUTRIENT ANALYSIS FOR ONE SERVING

Calories 163	**Carbohydrates** 25 g	**Total Fat** 5 g
Protein 3 g	**Fiber** 3 g	**Saturated Fat** <1 g
Sodium 194 mg	**Sugars** 3 g	**Monounsaturated Fat** 4 g
Cholesterol 18 mg		**Polyunsaturated Fat** <1 g

CHOCOLATE HAZELNUT BISCOTTI

FAT COUNT

5g

PERCENTAGE OF CALORIES

from total fat 27%

from saturated fat 3%

MAKES 24 COOKIES

These crunchy cookies are made for dunking. If you don't have hazelnuts on hand, chopped walnuts or sliced almonds are fine substitutes. Toast the hazelnuts using the method on page 138, then rub the nuts in a clean kitchen towel to remove the skins.

Preheat the oven to 325°F. Lightly coat a baking sheet with cooking spray.

Place the oats in a food processor and process to a fine powder.

In a large bowl, sift together the ground oats, flour, cocoa powder, baking soda, and salt.

In a blender or food processor, combine the honey, dates, oil, egg, and vanilla. Process until smooth. Make a well in the center of the dry ingredients and pour in the liquid mixture. Add the nuts to the well and stir just to combine; the dough will be sticky. Let stand for 15 minutes.

With damp hands, form the dough into two 10-inch logs. Place on the prepared baking sheet at least 4 inches apart. Flatten the logs to ³⁄₄-inch thickness. Bake until firm to the touch, about 20 minutes. Remove from the oven and let cool on the pan for 20 minutes. Reduce the oven temperature to 300°F.

Using a long serrated knife, cut the logs, still on the pan, on the diagonal into ¹⁄₂-inch-wide slices. Arrange the slices cut side down on the baking sheet and return to the oven for 10 minutes. Turn the slices and bake until the edges are golden, about 10 minutes longer. Let cool completely, then store in an airtight container.

Cooking spray

¾ cup old-fashioned rolled oats

1 cup unbleached all-purpose flour

½ cup unsweetened cocoa powder

½ teaspoon baking soda

¼ teaspoon salt

½ cup dark honey

½ cup pitted dates

3 tablespoons canola oil

1 egg

1 teaspoon vanilla extract

2 tablespoons hazelnuts or walnuts, toasted (page 138), skinned, and chopped

NUTRIENT ANALYSIS PER COOKIE

Calories 167	**Carbohydrates** 30 g	**Total Fat** 5 g
Protein 4 g	**Fiber** 1 g	**Saturated Fat** <1 g
Sodium 108 mg	**Sugars** 16 g	**Monounsaturated Fat** 3 g
Cholesterol 18 mg		**Polyunsaturated Fat** 1 g

PEANUT BUTTER & JAM COOKIES

PERCENTAGE OF CALORIES
from total fat   30%
from saturated fat   4%

MAKES ABOUT 24 COOKIES

Cooking spray

¾ cup natural unsalted peanut butter, stirred well before measuring

½ cup dark honey

½ cup nonfat vanilla yogurt

1 egg white

1½ teaspoons vanilla extract

1 cup all-purpose flour

½ cup whole-wheat flour

1 cup old-fashioned rolled oats

½ teaspoon baking soda

¼ teaspoon salt

¼ cup sugar-free jam or fruit spread

These moist cookies are reminiscent of the all-American lunchbox favorite. Strawberry, raspberry, or even blueberry jam makes a flavorful "thumbprint." Smooth or chunky peanut butter can be used.

Preheat the oven to 300°F. Lightly coat two baking sheets with cooking spray.

In a bowl, combine the peanut butter, honey, yogurt, egg white, and vanilla and beat with an electric mixer at medium speed until well blended, about 3 minutes. Add the flours, oats, baking soda, and salt and stir until well combined.

Using 2 level tablespoons per cookie, drop the dough 2 inches apart onto the prepared baking sheets and flatten slightly. Using the tip of your thumb, make an indent in the middle of each cookie. Spoon ½ teaspoon jam into each thumbprint.

Bake until the cookies are lightly browned at the edges, about 12 minutes. Transfer the cookies from the pans to wire racks to cool.

NUTRIENT ANALYSIS PER COOKIE

Calories 119	Carbohydrates 18 g	Total Fat 4 g
Protein 4 g	Fiber 1 g	Saturated Fat <1 g
Sodium 82 mg	Sugars 8 g	Monounsaturated Fat 2 g
Cholesterol <1 mg		Polyunsaturated Fat 1 g

POACHED PEARS WITH ORANGE-BERRY SAUCE

FAT COUNT

1 g

PERCENTAGE OF CALORIES
from total fat 4%
from saturated fat 0%

SERVES 8

This warm dessert is a great way to end a meal on a cool evening. The pears can also be made ahead and chilled for an easy summer treat.

Place the pear halves in a bowl with the lemon juice and toss gently to coat.

In a saucepan, combine 1 cup water, the wine, honey, orange juice, 1 tablespoon of the orange zest, the vanilla, cinnamon, and cloves. Bring to a boil over medium heat. Reduce to a simmer and add the pears and cranberries. Cover and simmer for about 3 minutes.

Remove from the heat and allow the pears to cool in the liquid. Using tongs, gently transfer the pears to a plate. Bring the poaching liquid to a boil and cook until reduced by half, about 4 minutes. In a blender or food processor, purée the reduced liquid with the blackberries. Transfer the pears to individual plates, spoon some sauce over each, and garnish with the remaining orange zest and the mint leaves, if desired.

4 firm but ripe Bosc pears, peeled, halved, and cored

2 tablespoons fresh lemon juice

1 cup dry white wine

¼ cup dark honey

2 tablespoons fresh orange juice

2 tablespoons grated orange zest

½ teaspoon vanilla extract

½ teaspoon ground cinnamon

Pinch of ground cloves

¼ cup chopped dried cranberries

2 cups blackberries

Fresh mint leaves for garnish (optional)

NUTRIENT ANALYSIS FOR ONE SERVING

Calories 125	**Carbohydrates** 27 g	**Total Fat** <1 g
Protein <1 g	**Fiber** 4 g	**Saturated Fat** 0 g
Sodium 2 mg	**Sugars** 20 g	**Monounsaturated Fat** 0 g
Cholesterol 0 mg		**Polyunsaturated Fat** 0 g

INGREDIENTS & TECHNIQUES

AL DENTE

Italian for "to the tooth," *al dente* refers to the firm texture traditionally desired in boiled dried pasta. It should not be hard at the center, but it should offer slight resistance when bitten. The best way to determine when it has reached this stage is by tasting the pasta near the end of its cooking time. Depending on its shape, most dried pasta requires 8 to 12 minutes of boiling.

BULGUR WHEAT

A staple in the Middle East, bulgur comes from whole wheat kernels that have been partially steamed, dried, and then cracked. It's widely available in a range of granulations, from a coarse grain for pilaf to a fine grinding for tabbouleh. Commonly used in salads, soups, and fillings, bulgur requires only brief soaking in water or a few minutes of cooking to bring out its nutty flavor.

BRAISING

This technique involves searing over high heat, then simmering in a covered pot. Browning and long cooking develop deep flavors, while low heat and moisture coax tougher cuts of meat into tenderness. Braising helps swell the starches in firm vegetables like carrots, winter squash, and sweet potatoes, and soften the fibers in dark greens such as kale and collards.

CAPERS

The flower buds of a spiny Mediterranean shrub, capers have a pleasantly pungent flavor. They lend a bright piquancy to a wide variety of sauces, salads, and dips. Although commonly available pickled in vinegar, capers that have been packed in salt retain the best flavor and texture. Briefly soak pickled capers or rinse salted ones in cold water to remove excess salt before using.

CHILES

A staple around the world, chiles—hot peppers—vary widely in shape, color, flavor, and heat levels. Most ripen from green to bright red, sweetening as they redden. Popular and versatile jalapeños register medium to hot. Poblanos are larger, slightly milder, and dark green to red-brown in color. Roast them first to bring out their smoky, earthy flavor and then add them to soups, stews, and sauces.

DARK HONEY

Depending on the blossoms or trees that bees visit while harvesting nectar and pollen, honey can vary widely in intensity of color and flavor. Honeys from avocado, chestnut, pumpkin, eucalyptus, or buckwheat flowers, or from wildflowers, are among the most popular of the dark varieties. They have assertive flavors with a hint of molasses and range in hue from pale amber to almost black.

COOKING DRIED BEANS

For the best texture, soak dried beans in water for at least 8 hours or overnight; drain and rinse. In a large pot, combine beans and water to cover by 2 inches. Bring the beans to a boil, cover partially, and simmer over low heat until tender, 40 to 50 minutes. Continue as directed in the recipe. Most varieties yield about 2½ to 3 cups cooked beans for every 1 cup dried.

DICING VEGETABLES

Cutting vegetables into even cubes creates visual appeal and promotes even cooking. Dice tiny cubes of bell pepper for garnishing or large chunks of potatoes for long simmering. In most recipes, ½-inch cubes serve well. To dice, first cut vegetables into thick slices with a large knife. Stack the slices, cut long pieces, then cut the pieces crosswise into cubes.

FLAXSEED

These tiny seeds, varying in color from pale gold to brown, have a nutty flavor that blends well in baked goods or cereals. For the best flavor and nutrient value, grind whole flaxseed in a coffee grinder, food processor, or blender. Whole flaxseed can be stored indefinitely at room temperature, but once ground, it should be kept in an airtight container in the refrigerator.

NUTMEG, WHOLE

Native to Indonesia, nutmeg has a warm, sweet-spicy flavor that marries well with spinach, fish, meat fillings, milk-based dishes, and many desserts. Because its aromatic oils dissipate quickly once the seed is ground, try to use whole nutmeg whenever possible. Although special nutmeg graters ensure the finest shavings, a fine-holed or hand-held rasp-type grater also works well.

LENTILS

A staple in the Middle East for 8,000 years, lentils are now available in dozens of types grown around the world. Varieties include the common brown lentil found in most supermarkets, dark green Le Puy lentils from France, yellow lentils from India, and the small red lentils of Egypt. Although always dried, they do not require presoaking and cook to tenderness in only 20 to 30 minutes.

OLIVE OIL

Essential to Mediterranean cuisine, olive oils can be bright green and peppery or mellow gold and slightly sweet. Extra-virgin olive oil, the highest quality grade, retains the most color and flavor, but it's best reserved for sauces and quick sautés, as it loses character at even moderate temperatures. Regular olive oil, lighter in flavor and color, holds up well to high-heat cooking such as grilling.

PEELING MANGOES

To peel and dice a ripe mango, stand the fruit on one of its narrow ends. Cut the mango off-center, just grazing one side of the pit. Repeat on the other side. Score the cut side of the two lobes in a grid without piercing the peel. Press the mango lobes inside out and slice off the cubes of fruit near the peel. Finally, remove the peel from the fruit around the pit, then cut the fruit away from the pit.

SESAME OIL

Made from toasted sesame seeds, dark sesame oil has a rich amber color and an intense, nutty flavor. Clear, refined sesame oils are better for high-heat cooking, but dark oils offer more flavor, even in tiny amounts. Look for them in Asian markets or in the ethnic or international aisle of supermarkets. More perishable than other oils, dark sesame oil is best stored in the refrigerator.

PORTOBELLO MUSHROOMS

The dark brown, wide caps of portobello mushrooms are excellent roasted or grilled whole for filling sandwiches or topping creamy polenta. To sauté portobellos, cut the caps into thick slices. They require only a light misting with olive oil and a sprinkle of salt and pepper to bring out their flavor. Twist the stems carefully to remove without breaking the caps.

SHALLOTS

Diminutive members of the onion family, shallots grow in small clusters much like garlic. Their papery, reddish brown skin covers white flesh tinged with pink or purple. Although layered like onions, with a similar strong aroma, they are valued for their more delicate flavor, which is especially good in sauces and vinaigrettes. Keep shallots in a cool, dark, well-ventilated place.

SOYBEANS, FRESH

Also known as edamame, soybeans picked still in their pods retain a bright green color and a fresh, nutty flavor. Left whole, they can be boiled or steamed for a snack. Shelled, they're enjoyed much like English peas in vegetable dishes, soups, or purées. Look for soybeans during summer in produce markets or year-round in the freezers of natural-food stores and many large supermarkets.

SWEET POTATOES

Although often confused with yams, sweet potatoes have a sweeter flavor and less starchy flesh. They are excellent baked whole, roasted or braised with a honey or maple syrup glaze, or mashed with a touch of cinnamon or nutmeg. Shop for sweet potatoes free of dark blemishes. Store in a cool, dark, well-ventilated place but avoid refrigerating them, as cold temperatures will alter their flavor.

SPECIALTY VINEGARS

French for "sour wine," vinegar forms when bacteria turn a fermented liquid into a weak solution of acetic acid. Red wine, white wine, balsamic, and sherry vinegars are among the best for cooking, as they display traits of the wines from which they are made, along with a sourness that makes them valuable in balancing flavors. Look for top-quality, unfiltered aged vinegars.

TOASTING NUTS

Cooking nuts until they are golden deepens their flavor and improves their texture. You can toast nuts by baking them on a cookie sheet in a 325°F oven or by stirring them in a small, dry, nonstick frying pan over medium-high heat. Cook them just until they're fragrant and golden in color, about 10 minutes. Take care not to overcook them, as they will become bitter when scorched.

TOFU

Soy milk, made from cooked soybeans, forms tofu when curdled and pressed into blocks. Although bland, tofu readily absorbs flavors from marinades and sauces. The smooth texture of silken tofu is ideal for puréeing and for adding body to soups. Firm tofu, denser and coarser in texture, holds together well for stir-frying and grilling. To store tofu, submerge it in cold water and refrigerate.

WHEAT BRAN AND WHEAT GERM

During the milling of wheat, the kernel's outer covering, known as the bran, and its tiny embryo, the germ, are usually both removed. Sold in natural-food stores and most supermarkets, wheat bran and wheat germ add nutrient value to cereals, casseroles, fillings, and baked goods. Unless the germ is defatted, it should be stored in an airtight container in the refrigerator.

VINAIGRETTE

Making a vinaigrette involves little more than whisking together a small amount of oil, vinegar, salt, pepper, and perhaps an aromatic ingredient such as garlic, shallots, a dab of prepared mustard, or some minced fresh herbs. In addition to dressing salads, a vinaigrette can be used as a marinade before roasting, a basting liquid at the grill, or a sauce for steamed vegetables.

ZEST

The thin outer peel of citrus fruits, known as the zest, is rich in aromatic oils. A fine-holed or rasp-type grater will shred the zest into delicate shavings for marinades or rubs. Use a zester to create thin, elegant strips for garnish. Take care not to cut or grate into the white, pulpy pith that lies just beneath the outer peel, as it has a spongy texture and an unpleasantly bitter flavor.

INDEX

MEREDITH® BOOKS

Editor in Chief: Linda Raglan Cunningham

Publisher: James D. Blume
Executive Director, Marketing: Jeffrey Myers
Executive Director, New Business Development: Todd M. Davis
Executive Director, Sales: Ken Zagor
Director, Operations: George A. Susral
Director, Production: Douglas M. Johnston
Business Director: Jim Leonard

Vice President and General Manager: Douglas J. Guendel

Meredith Publishing Group
President, Publishing Group: Stephen M. Lacy
Vice President-Publishing Director: Bob Mate

Meredith Corporation
Chairman and Chief Executive Officer: William T. Kerr

In Memoriam: E.T. Meredith III (1933–2003)

AMERICAN MEDICAL ASSOCIATION

Executive Vice President,
    Chief Executive Officer: Michael D. Maves, M.D.
Senior Vice President,
    Publishing and Business Services: Robert A. Musacchio, Ph.D.
Vice President, Business Products: Anthony J. Frankos
Chief Operations Officer, AMA Press: Mary Lou White
Managing Editor: Donna Kotulak
Writer: Pam Brick
Editors: Robin Husayko, Steve Michaels
Copy Editor: Reuben Rios
Art Editor: Mary Ann Albanese
Medical Editor: Bonnie Chi-Lum, M.D., M.P.H.
Contributing Editor: Maryellen Westerberg, Dr.P.H., R.D., C.D.E.
Consultants: Clair M. Callan, M.D., Thomas Houston, M.D.

The recommendations and information in this book are appropriate in most cases and current as of the date of publication. For specific information, concerning your or a family member's medical condition, the AMA suggests that you consult a physician.

WELDON OWEN INC.

Chief Executive Officer: John Owen
President and Chief Operating Officer: Terry Newell
Vice President International Sales: Stuart Laurence
Creative Director: Gaye Allen
Associate Creative Director: Leslie Harrington
Associate Publisher: Val Cipollone
Managing Editor: Sheridan Warrick
Designer: Leon Yu
Editorial Assistants: Mitch Goldman, Juli Vendzules
Copy Editor and Proofreader: Carrie Bradley and Desne Ahlers
Indexer: Ken DellaPenta
Production Director: Chris Hemesath
Color Specialist: Teri Bell
Production Coordinator: Todd Rechner

The American Medical Association Healthy Heart Cookbook
Conceived and produced by Weldon Owen Inc.
814 Montgomery Street, San Francisco, CA 94133
Telephone: 415-291-0100 Fax: 415-291-8841

First printed in 2004
10 9 8 7 6 5 4 3 2 1

ISBN: 0-696-22151-9
Printed by Midas Printing Limited, China

Acknowledgments
Thanks to Kyrie Forbes, Karin Skaggs, Joan Olson, and Robin Terra for design assistance; Joseph De Leo for art direction; Suzette Kaminsky, Kim Konecny, Erin Quon, and Dan Becker for food styling; Joe Maer and Leigh Noë for prop styling; Kevin Kerr and Selena Aument for assisting in the studio; and Heather Dunn, Gina Bessire, Tanya Henry, and Jackie Mancuso for modeling.

Photographs by Sheri Giblin: pages 9 (bottom left and right), 13 (three at left), 14 (middle at right), 15, 16 (three at right), 23, 25 (third from top), 26, 48, 52, 100.